The Illustrated Garden Planter

Diana Saville

Illustrations by Fenja Gunn

ALLEN LANE

ALLEN LANE
Penguin Books Ltd
536 King's Road
London SW10 0UH

First published 1984
Conceived, edited and designed by Robert Ditchfield Books

ISBN 0 7139 1480 7

Printed and bound in Great Britain by
William Clowes Limited, Beccles and London

Contents

Introduction

This book is more than a catalogue of garden plants. Rather, its purpose is to act as an illustrated guide to plantings in different forms of gardens. Its intention is to simplify that most complex part of garden-making which consists of choosing appropriate plants for any position and planning their combinations. For it is in the putting together that the picture so often comes apart.

The following pages are divided into three main sections; the first on terraces and courtyards, the second on beds and borders and the last on hedges, backgrounds and features. Within this framework, ranges of plants are presented in groups according to their attributes and their suitability to a particular setting. Some interrelation is inevitable and certain key plants may crop up in two or even all three sections, for there are many subjects which can be put to multiple use, equally suited, for example, to embossing a paved terrace or, alternatively, forming a carpet at the foot of a hedge.

In effect, then, this collection of plants can be used as a kit from which millions of individual combinations, some exaggeratedly simple or others of rococo complexity, might be assembled. Eight such combinations are shown here in the form of gardens, exhibited both before and after planting, which demonstrate the precise way in which plants have been chosen and assembled – sometimes to emphasise advantages, often to solve problems and simply to furnish. These example gardens underline a fact which cannot be stressed enough; that the impact of plants is almost always collective. Plants are usually seen in association with each other and they have to be chosen so that they are in harmony not only with their habitat but with their neighbours.

Nearly 650 plants have been illustrated in detail here, and in all over 900 described. The choice is partly a personal one yet based on much else besides. Floral beauty, perfume, grace of leaf, trunk and habit, distinction, suitability for a particular pupose, ease of temperament, all these factors have played their part singly or in combination. Yet, to add a personal note, I have also thought it important that this corps d'élite should keep recondite plants to a minimum and, to this end, have tried to hold the balance in favour of more easily available plants, for planning a garden is dispiriting if all one's choices prove elusive. With the same aim in mind, I have designed the gardens to contain mostly plants which are usually obtainable from good garden centres.

In each case the approximate height of a plant has been given as a guide. Spread varies so greatly according to area, soil, climate and position that, in trees and shrubs particularly, measurements can mislead rather than help. Nonetheless, where a tree or shrub is normally wider than tall, a measurement of width is provided on the basis that any guide is better than none in such cases. With herbaceous plants, both height and width are given, the second of the two figures referring chiefly to the approximate (close) planting distance. The following symbols are also used throughout the book and they refer to all plants mentioned within the paragraph unless otherwise stated.

E = evergreen
○ = thrives best or only in full sun
◑ = thrives best or only in part-shade
● = succeeds in full shade
LH will not tolerate or thrive in a chalky or limy earth and prefers or must have acid, peaty soil to succeed.

At the head of each group of plants is a small 'map' of the garden in which selected plants from that page have been used. These plants are detailed on the map to assist identification.

The full planting key to each garden is given at the end of the relevant section.

Finally, a note about nomenclature. For ease of reference, I have given the botanical name under which a plant is most widely listed for the general gardener, but these names are sometimes changed and in such cases, I have provided the new name or synonym beside the old.

How to use this Book

To Find Plants

You may have a clear idea of what you need plants for – to cover a wall, creep between paving, provide colour throughout summer etc. This book illustrates and describes 34 categories of plants; turn to the one you need and you will find a variety to choose from. By referring back to the example garden illustrated in that category, you will also be able to see how such plants can be used in an overall design.

To Plant a Garden

If you want to plant an area, you can use as a guide the example garden in this book which resembles most closely the features and problems of your own. You can consider the planting solutions given in the example garden as possibilities for yourself, and if you refer to the pages from which the plants have been selected, you will find many other candidates which will fulfil the same role.

Plants for Terraces and Courtyards

Plants for Terraces and Courtyards

A terrace or a courtyard is the sole architectural feature which is essential in most gardens. It has a utilitarian function: to allow the owner to sit, eat and entertain in an area which is adjacent and convenient to the house. Yet it has an aesthetic and ideal function too, which is to ease the house in stages into the garden beyond, a purpose it fulfils by combining masonry and plants.

Here more than elsewhere, masonry has the upper hand over plants. It is not a place for confusion and plants cannot enjoy the relatively unfettered freedom that may be theirs in wilder or more spacious parts of the garden. Nonetheless they are essential and usually under-used ingredients which will soften and decorate the harsh architectural contours and bring movement and change to the static surface.

It is easier to plan if you visualise it as an area with a clear centre, spacious enough to allow room for your activities or relaxation and for features such as a specimen tree for shade or a small formal pool. Plants can surf forwards luxuriantly over the edges of this area, some rocketing upwards to give vertical contrast to the horizontal lines, others (outside the main traffic lines) encrusting the surface and even encroaching abundantly so long as this does not cause complications. Potted plants can be placed where they cannot grow in the earth and positioned to give a visual balance to other areas as in Garden 3 on p. 14.

This garden and both the other examples immediately overleaf demonstrate the way these particular terraces and courtyards have been arranged to overcome individual problems. The plants used in these gardens have been taken almost entirely from this first section of the book, and you will find these plants presented in groups up to p. 41. The introductory remarks to each group are a guide to their general purpose and use, but when sifting them for your own terrace or courtyard, remember to choose plants in scale with your surroundings, a point that applies to plant size, outline and even leaves. And remember too that on a drowsy afternoon or at the stillness of dusk, it is the scented flowers that will give you so much pleasure here.

Garden 1

Small and Narrow

This kind of enclosed town garden presents certain typical difficulties which arise partly from the nature of the site and partly from the degree of neglect. The owner's best hope of tackling the problems is to define them individually, so that he can then decide on step-by-step solutions which will involve, in this case, both structural alterations and clever planting.

1. There is insufficient space for a lawn as well as a patio, and the existing concrete is, anyway, the most unsympathetic material for this.
2. The smallness of the garden and the height of its walls make it seem an oppressive box or backyard.
3. The plain brick walls have a harsh, hard appearance.
4. There is no shade near the house in the hottest part of the day.
5. Two eyesores need to be concealed; the dustbin and the shed.

Solutions

1. As the garden is too small for a proper lawn, treat it all as a courtyard. Paving slabs can replace the concrete and grass, leaving areas uncovered for plants.
2. The size of the garden can be camouflaged, firstly, by installing a door in the end wall (which suggests the garden is larger than it is) and, secondly, by concealing the boundaries with climbers. Lavish planting will convert it from a boxy backyard into a garden. BULBS (pages 32–33) are especially valuable in a small area for they take up little room.
3. These high brick walls need softening. CLIMBERS (pages 20–21) and shrubs will do this. Also, a selection of ARCHITECTURAL PLANTS (pages 26–27) with their bold leaves and outlines will stand out against all the masonry.
4. A pergola erected near the house and planted with suitable climbing plants will give shade where it is most needed. Two vines are chosen to cover it, one bearing edible fruit so that it is useful as well as decorative.
5. EVERGREENS (pages 22–23) and a deciduous climber conceal the eyesores. The evergreens will keep the garden clothed in winter if they are also planted around the whole area.
The picture shows the garden in full summer. Planting plan on page 42.

Garden 2

Dark and Dank

This suburban garden has plenty of scope for family life as it is large enough to be divided into separate areas for different purposes. Children can use the grass for play, so need not encroach on the yard at the back of the house where the owners would like to form an attractive view from the windows. This yard, however, poses problems as an ornamental area.

1. It receives little sun. It faces north-west and even late sun is partly blocked by buildings and trees.
2. The neglected crazy paving is overgrown with weeds.
3. It will be the only ornamental area, but there is little room to grow flowers in variety.
4. It has permanently difficult areas; for example, damp patches by the gutters of house and shed, and, in contrast, dry shade under the conifers.

Solutions

1. In an area as dark as this, shade-tolerant GOLD AND BRIGHT GREEN PLANTS in quantity (pages 28–29) are vital to give the effect of sunlight. If a fair proportion of these are evergreen, the yard will remain equally bright in winter.

2. The crazy-paving has outgrown its life. The easiest solution is to replace it with gravel over a layer of black polythene (page 16) and by beds for GROUND-COVER PLANTS (pages 34–35). Both will help to control weeds in future and make for easy maintenance.

3. Since there is so little room for flowers, it would be reasonable to choose those that stay in bloom for a prolonged period, even under these conditions. See LONG-SEASON FLOWERS (pages 36–37) for a selection.

4. PLANTS FOR DIFFICULT SPOTS (pages 38–39) come to the rescue here also. Those that tolerate drip can be planted by the gutters; others that endure dry shade will be suitable near the thuja trees. The plants immediately below these conifers, such as the golden ivies, will need feeding when planted and annual nourishment if they are to perform well in such adverse conditions.

The picture shows the garden in late spring. Planting plan on page 43.

Garden 3

Open Expanse of Paving

Few terraces are more functional but less ornamental than this type which is often seen beside a post-war house or bungalow. It is streamlined for modern convenience and provides plenty of room for sitting, eating and entertaining, yet the surroundings are bleak. The drawbacks are obvious:

1. Low fences form the boundary to the garden with the result that there is an entire lack of privacy.
2. The uninterrupted expanse of paving is monotonous and lifeless. This is the crudest and least imaginative form of terrace.
3. There is no variation in height on the terrace, an additional reason why it looks so dull.
4. The whole area will bake in sun, for heat will be intensified by the paving.

Solutions

1. The quickest way of achieving seclusion in this terrace is to raise the low fences with trellis or with netting erected on uprights. Climbers, tall shrubs and several SMALL TREES (pages 18–19) can then hide these supports.

2. Some of the paving slabs can be lifted. If the soil is heavy and moist beneath, it will have to be replaced with light, friable earth to a depth of about 20cm above the broken-up sub-soil. PAVING CREEPERS (pages 24–25) can then fill these spaces. A selection can also grow in earth around the sides of a few non-traffic-bearing slabs. Other paving slabs can be replaced by cobbles which will enliven the appearance of the ground.

3. SMALL TREES will play the major part in varying the heights on this terrace. If several of these can be grown within the cobbled areas, it will make the patterned masonry seem more purposeful. Pots and tubs of plants (see TEMPORARY EFFECTS on pages 40–41) will also boost the interest and variety.

4. GREY AND SILVER PLANTS (pages 30–31) are stalwart in full sun and very dry conditions. Nearly all will benefit from the good drainage that is likely in conditions such as these.

The picture shows the garden in autumn. Planting plan on page 44.

Planning and Making a Paved Area

Rule one is to ponder at length before making a terrace. Unlike beds, borders, lawns and most other components of a garden, it is a fixture and in consequence demands considerable forethought. Mistakes are ineradicable except at great cost and effort.

As a start, decide whether you want a terrace or a courtyard or a cross between the two. A courtyard is enclosed on at least three sides, whereas in contrast, a terrace, defined as a raised level area, enjoys an open vista to garden and landscape beyond. Yet in practice, it too may benefit from partial self-containment in the interests of privacy and shelter, for seclusion and repose are the cardinal requirements of this type of garden.

Consider, also, the question of its place within the garden. In very small gardens, these paved areas, enclosed or otherwise, may represent the garden in its entirety (as in Garden 1). In larger gardens, they will only be part of the whole and in this setting, it is conventional to position them on an axial line from the doors and windows of the garden front of the house. Convenience as well as the appeal of views from the house play their part here. But in certain cases, sometimes from lack of choice or where there is more space at the side and equal ease of access, more sunlight, less wind, greater privacy and a finer outlook (as in Garden 7 on p.84), there are arguments for constructing the terrace in this less orthodox position.

Once the setting is agreed, work out exactly what you need in terms of privacy, space, shade, screens against eyesores, traffic lines and, not least, plants, for which spaces may need to be left free in the paving. A small pool is one possible requirement (see p. 72) and a hedge may be necessary for shelter and privacy (p. 81 onwards). A dry-stone wall (p. 76) could give some security at the edge of a raised terrace as well as provide extra space for plants.

Choice of materials

Cost, convenience, ease of maintenance and suitability in colour and texture to the adjacent house are all factors which will influence your choice of surface materials. There are seven main possibilities.

Paving Paving slabs can be artificial or natural, the latter being much more expensive. Both are obtainable in a wide range of sizes and colours, but avoid the ice-cream coloured extremes of the artificial slabs and choose an unobtrusive fawn or grey which will weather more comfortably. A roughened texture to the surface, simulating the flaking of natural stone, is also preferable and more slip-proof. If the paving borders a step and its edges are exposed, choose pavers which simulate the worn edges of natural stone.

Slates A less commonly used material, usually in greyish-green but also dusky blue. Looks its best when it can be incorporated in discrete bands or edging strips, where it forms a subtle rather than startling contrast with the main paving. It is strong and durable and can be bought in random sizes, usually squares or rectangles.

Granite setts A much smaller unit than either of the above varying from 15cm square to 40cm × 20cm. Natural or artificial, and normally grey or a blend of rusts, they form attractive panels or insertions and can be used as relief areas like the cobble stones in Garden 3. Used on their own in a large terrace, they are less distracting if their pattern is broken up at intervals by plantings.

Bricks Old bricks have a softer warmth than new, though there are a few exceptions to this. If old, they must be in good condition, frost-proof, free or freeable of mortar, suitable for external use. Colours vary enormously from grey, donkey brown, rust to fawn, but avoid any of the glaring yellows. A good subject by an old brick house or where paths from the terrace are also old brick. As small units, they can be laid to form curves or irregular lines.

Quarry tiles have a domesticated appearance and are best confined to the area immediately beside the house, perhaps within a verandah or beneath a balcony. Square or hexagonal, they range from terracotta to blue to grey-green.

Cobblestones Highly decorative when alternating with slabs as in Garden 3, but a difficult surface for wheelbarrows, prams, trolleys etc. so they must be kept away from the traffic lines of the terrace.

Gravel This material consists simply of stone chippings in sizes from 2·5cm to 6mm, a pea-sized gravel so small it will stick to shoe soles and be walked into the house. Shades include pinks, rusts, grey-green, buff and grey. It is cheap, easy to lay and a first choice where a surface cannot be accurately levelled. It does not need maintenance as such, but unless it is laid over polythene (see p. 16) it will become infested with weeds. It will also need intermittent raking to keep it evenly distributed.

Two surfaces are better avoided if possible. **Crazy paving**, especially when mortared, is distracting to the eye and discordant in a disciplined setting. **Concrete** is never suitable; as a working surface only, it is a clumsy intruder into any ornamental area.

Costing the operation

Calculate paving slabs, slates, setts and quarry tiles from a scale drawing of the area. Bricks are usually supplied in multiples of 100; very roughly, 35 laid flat cover a square yard. Err on the generous side in your estimate. Builders merchants will give guidance on cobblestones and gravel for a given area and can also help in calculating sand and ballast.

Clearing the site

Clear deeply enough to ensure that when the area is paved and bedded, the surface will rest at least 15cm below the damp-proof course of the house. Level the site but make a very slight slope (a minimum of 2·5cm in 2·5m, or 2·5cm in 1·2m in large terraces) away from the house so that rain does not collect there. Save topsoil for plant areas.

Laying the materials

Paving slabs If the ground is soft, roll in 10cm hardcore topped with a fine material like ashes or sand. Check level. Bed slabs in a mix of 1 part cement and 6 parts sand to a depth of 2·5cm in traffic area. To the sides of the terrace or where it will be planted, use this mix in dabs under each corner and in the middle of the slabs. Keep lines straight with pegs and string. Tap slabs into position using a hammer with a block of wood over the slabs to prevent damage. Fill joints with sandy earth for planting, or on traffic lines brush 1 part cement to 3 parts sand into the joints and water with a fine-rosed watering can.

Slates Excavate 8·5cm (or 13·5 cm depending on depth of slates, steadiness of soil and heaviness of traffic) and lay 5cm deep (or 10cm deep) concrete base (a mix of 1 part cement, 3 parts fine sand, 6 parts 10mm aggregate). Top with 2·5cm mortar bed (see mix under paving slabs) and bed slates.

Granite setts Prepare base as for paving slabs but make the mortar bed 5cm deep. Put setts into bed before it hardens. Finish by brushing cement and sand into joints and watering as in paving slabs.

Bricks Treat as for paving slabs, using rubble or hardcore topped with ashes or sand. Either bed the bricks in 2·5cm deep mortar (see mix under paving slabs) or dry-lay the bricks on a consolidated ash bed. Fill the 1cm joints with sand or point on traffic lines with a mortar of 1 part lime and 4 parts soft sand. Wash off any mortar that stains the surface at once.

Quarry tiles See instructions on **Slate** but point as for **Bricks**.

Cobblestones Bed the stones in a mortar base over hardcore as given under **Paving slabs**, but the mortar base should be 7·5cm deep. Cobbles should be sunk into the bed before it hardens to at least half their own depth. Work with the cobbles sitting in a bucket of water to stop them drying out.

Gravel Put down a layer of sand over 10cm depth of hardcore and then pour in at least two separate layers of gravel to the thickness of 3·7cm. Water each layer, ram and rake even. If you want to avoid weeds, cover the sand with a sheet of black polythene before adding the gravel, but not in areas where you risk starving tree roots. You can plant at any time by cutting holes in the polythene and scooping out the hardcore etc. below and making earth pockets here, but confine your plants to those which will tolerate such conditions.

Assessing and preparing the soil

Soil is either acid, neutral or alkaline, expressed in what is called the pH scale. Its acidity or alkalinity matters because lime-intolerant plants (such as rhododendrons, some heaths, camellias etc.) will not thrive in an alkaline soil. You can buy soil-testing kits which will assess your soil type.

In other respects, certain soil-types are recognisable by their textures and should be treated accordingly. 1) Sandy soil is light, gritty and dries out quickly. Add peat or compost to improve its ability to hold moisture. 2) Chalky soil is shallow and sometimes has lumps of chalk or limestone in its subsoil. Add compost or rotted manure and fertilisers. 3) Clay soil is heavy and sticky in winter like plasticine, yet dries out in summer to concrete. Dig it over roughly in the autumn to allow frosts to break it down and add strawy compost or organic matter. If the clay is very heavy, add garden lime (375gms per sq. metre) over dry soil. Don't add any fertilisers for at least one month before liming and for three months afterwards. Also, liming means you cannot grow lime-intolerant plants in the soil, nor even in those areas into which the soil or water might leach to any extent.

Designing with plants

Generally speaking, it is easier to place plants attractively around a paved area than it is in the more open parts of a garden. For one reason, the area is usually a small one and the disposition of its space is the less challenging as a result. For another reason, an architectural framework is normally present, forcing the design to conform to some extent to its geometric discipline. Nonetheless, it is perilous to rely on these aids to the extent of ignoring certain other maxims. Some of these are covered in the introductions to the following spreads, but the three most important concern height, colour and foliage.

Variation of height is vital on a terrace. This means including one or more trees if at all possible (see pages 18–19 and page 55) which will also help to break the abrupt transition between the tall house and the ground level.

Secondly, evergreen foliage on a very high proportion of the plants is equally essential if the area is visible from the house throughout the year as is usually the case (see pages 22–23).

As for colour, it is better to keep the palette subtle rather than dazzling. View with suspicion hot colours which are disturbing to the eye in a limited area on view the whole time. Choose either a restricted colour combination as in Garden 2, or, for more showy effects, the kind of wide chromatic range as in Garden 1. This, though brightly coloured, avoids hot oranges and scarlets, the brightest blues and too much egg-yolk yellow. The deeper reds and purples and also some dark-foliaged plants help to stabilise the light, fresh greens. White is used for illumination.

It is worth adding, however, that on a terrace especially, a design cannot depend on colour alone in the manner of a flower border. Its pattern should be apparent even in black and white (as in Garden 3); and it may help to sketch one's own design in advance with a pen, or photograph the area and draw in the planting plan, assessing by this method whether the design measures up to this monotone test.

Planting

The planting season for bare-rooted deciduous trees and shrubs is from November to March, but if the soil is frozen, very sticky or sodden when the plants arrive, make an earth trench in some spare ground and 'heel in' the plants until conditions improve. Evergreens are better planted in either early autumn or mid-spring when the soil is warmer. Container-grown plants can be planted at any time of the year. Soak the root ball well before removing the polythene and planting. All new plants must be watered regularly during dry spells for up to a year after planting.

Where each tree, shrub or plant will grow, prepare a flat-bottomed hole deeper and wider than the roots will occupy. Put rotted manure or compost right at the base and cover with good topsoil (so that the roots cannot touch the manure). Place the plant in position, pouring damp peat mixed with a little bonemeal around the roots. Don't plant deeper than the soil mark on the stem (with the exception of clematis; see p. 21). Firm the soil over the roots when they are covered and re-firm after a heavy frost. Secure planting is always essential.

Trees need a stake placed stoutly in position before the roots are inserted in the hole. Tie the stem to the stake with a soft rubber or cloth tie which will not chafe the bark.

Water all new plants well to settle in, and thereafter keep free of weeds. In dry weather or drying winds, young conifers may need their foliage regularly sprayed as well as their roots watered.

In all cases, a mulch (see page 53) will help to prevent the newly planted subjects from drying out before their roots can establish themselves. But if planting in the depth of winter when the soil is cold, wait until spring before applying the material. Time it so that the soil is still moist but beginning to warm.

Small Trees

A small tree is a substantial asset in all but the tiniest courtyards, bestowing shade near a house and effecting a change of height which is always essential to engage interest. And if it is planted to the side of the courtyard and allowed to overhang slightly one of the walls or fences, it will also help to dispel the feeling of claustrophobia sometimes induced by small enclosures.

Since it will be the most dominant plant on the terrace, the tree deserves to be chosen with care. Perhaps spectacular flowers at one season are the most important feature, or a beautifully marked bark which will look handsome throughout the year. A graceful evergreen tree may be preferable whose leaves help to keep the garden clothed at all seasons. Or instead will a tree be needed to bear edible fruit? If the courtyard is gravelled, bear in mind that small leaves are difficult to pick up when shed. A further selection of trees can be found on page 55.

TREES FOR SPRING EFFECT

Magnolia × soulangiana LH: ○ (1) The most popular and adaptable of the magnolias with spectacular, goblet-shaped flowers in spring before the leaves open. It is tolerant of clay soils and atmospheric pollution. There are a number of fine clones, including **'Alba'** (with white flowers), **'Lennei'** (the outside of the flower is rosy-purple), **'Rustica Rubra'** (the outside is rosy-crimson) and **'Brozzoni'** with especially large white flowers bearing a purple stain at the base. The tree is usually rather shrubby and wide-spreading. 7m.

Malus floribunda (2) The low, bushy, very broad-headed Japanese crab-apple tree bearing masses of small flowers which are rosy-red in bud and pink fading to white when open. Small red and yellow fruits in autumn. 5m × 6m.

***Prunus* 'Accolade'** (3) A beautiful member of a family which are all excellent subjects for limy soil. 'Accolade' has spreading branches and semi-double flowers of the richest pink, opening in early spring. The leaves usually colour red and orange in autumn. 6m.

FLOWERING TREES FOR OTHER SEASONS

Eucryphia glutinosa LH: ◑ (4) A shrubby tree making a glorious display in July-August with its massed, 6cm wide white, yellow-stamened, scented blossoms. Its dark green, pinnate leaves colour richly in autumn before falling. It is not suitable for chalky or limy soil. 4m.

Koelreuteria paniculata ○ (5) A domed, picturesque tree with branching panicles up to 40cm long of golden flowers in August. Its long, dark green pinnate leaves open as deep red in late spring and turn yellow in autumn. Full sun is preferable and it will perform best in warm, dry summers. 10m.

***Prunus subhirtella* 'Autumnalis'** (6) A most valuable tree near a

house for its winter beauty. Its delicate white (or palest pink in the form **'Rosea'**) bell-shaped flowers open in small, intermittent flushes from late October throughout the winter, the remainder blooming in spring. Spreading, densely-twigged crown. 6m.

Styrax japonica LH (7) A tree which is best sited where it can be viewed from beneath for its white flowers, like snowdrops, are borne in June on the underside of its branches. Wide-spreading, rather rounded crown. It grows best in lime-free soil with peat or compost to retain moisture. Needs shelter and part shade in warm areas. 8m.

TREES WITH SPECIAL FEATURES

Acer pensylvanicum (8) The light greyish-green bark with arresting white stripes is the attraction of this tree. The olive green leaves turn gold in autumn. Rather inconspicuous flowers on pink racemes in spring. Not for chalk. 12m.

Paulownia tomentosa (syn. *P. imperialis*) (9) Tree of very rapid growth, making a domed crown. The rich green leaves are large (up to 35cm) and must have shelter from wind in case they are torn. The mauve, foxglove-shaped flowers give a fine display in May, if the buds have not been frosted when they start to open. 10m.

Pinus pinea E (10) This is the Stone Pine, the very dark umbrella-shaped conifer which is a characteristic feature in Mediterranean countries. Very slow-growing, but its shape is so picturesque when mature that it is worth considering. 10m.

Prunus serrula (11) A vigorous tree with a polished mahogany-red bark which is handsome at all times of the year. Dullish green leaves which tend to hide the mass of very small white flowers in late spring. 8m.

Prunus subhirtella **'Pendula'** (12) Forms an extraordinary, spreading hummock whose pendulous branches are fascinating even in winter bareness. Flowers in spring are blush-white, or pink in the form **'Rosea'** or deep rose in the clone **'Rubra'**. Needs a great deal of lateral space. 5m × 7m.

FRUITING TREES

Arbutus unedo E (13) Darkish-red bark, dark evergreen leaves, and highly ornamental strawberry-like fruits in late autumn at the same time as the white flower-bells open. The form **'Rubra'** has pinkish flowers. (The fruit is edible but unpalatable.) 10m.

Fig tree ○ (14) **'Brown Turkey'** is the most reliable fruiting clone for outdoor culture in northern climates, where it should ripen one crop a year in a warm, sheltered position. Very glossy, deep green ornamental leaves of architectural value. 6m. See also p. 27.

Malus **'Eleyi'** (15) Crab apple with wine-red flowers in late spring and purple-red 2·5cm fruit in autumn. Purplish juvenile foliage, ageing to bronze-green. 6m.

Malus **'Golden Hornet'** (16) White flowers in late spring precede rounded, golden fruits. 4m spreading tree. One of the best crabs for jelly-making as is the cultivar **'John Downie'** with orange and scarlet fruits. 8m.

Mespilus germanica (17) The Medlar is picturesque and wide-spreading with large, hairy leaves turning russet in autumn. The white flowers in late spring are followed by brown fruits in autumn, edible when over-ripe. 9m.

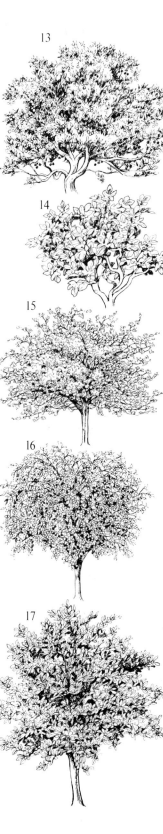

Climbers

Climbing plants support themselves, whether by aerial roots or by adhesive pads or by twining stems (or leaf stems) or by spines on their long arching shoots which hook into and over objects in their path. Others are not strictly speaking climbers, but will shove and lean their way up a wall, or can be trained by securing their stems to wires or trellis. All these different types are indispensable for hiding unsightly boundaries or buildings, whether walls, fences, screens or sheds. Festoon these eyesores with colour and foliage, and you have a vertical garden instead. Climbers are also key plants for providing privacy, and if they are grown against a trellis or netting erected above a low wall, they will give a high degree of seclusion. Plan their position carefully, relating their ultimate height and vigour of growth to the situation they will occupy. This is important, because it is not so simple to rid yourself of a mistake when the plant has covered the wall. (See also pp. 29, 56, 96–97 and 104–105.)

EVERGREENS

Berberidopsis corallina E:LH: ● (3) Leathery dark leaves and crimson flowers in late summer on drooping stems or racemes. Rather tender and demands shady, sheltered position and cool, lime-free soil. Tie leading shoots to support. 6m.

Clematis armandii E:○ (4) Trifoliate leaves and scented flowers in spring which are white in the form **'Snowdrift'** and blush in the cultivar **'Apple Blossom'**. Vigorous to 4m but a sheltered, sunny wall is essential. Provide support.

Honeysuckle **Lonicera japonica 'Halliana'** E (5) is rampant in growth, but redeemed by its evergreen leaves (semi-evergreen in a hard winter) and fragrant, white ageing to yellow flowers from June onwards. Provide support. Prune firmly. Up to 10m.

Ivy E Self-clinging, varied, usually quick-growing and tough climbers which are indispensable for a shady wall, though most will also grow well in sun. One of the boldest is the dark green **Hedera colchica 'Dentata'** (1) shown here in its cream-splashed form **'Variegata'**. 10m. **H. helix 'Cristata'** (2) is smaller with pale green crinkled leaves. 4m. See also *H.h.* 'Goldheart' on p. 28, and *H.h.* 'Glacier' on p. 96.

ROSES

Of the easily obtainable cultivars, the following are fine representatives of the different colour ranges. Tie all to supports on a wall.

'Allen Chandler' (10) Large, semi-double, crimson blooms mainly in June but recurrently thereafter. Fragrant. Good subject for north walls. 5m.

'Mermaid' (9) Loveliest of the yellows with large, single flowers all summer and semi-evergreen leaves. Needs ample space and a sheltered wall. Do not prune. 9m.

'Mme. Alfred Carrière' (11) A sweetly scented and perpetual-flowering rose with double blush-white flowers and disease-free foliage. Also good for north walls. 6m.

'Mme. Grégoire Staechelin' (7) Once-blooming only in early summer but impressive display of large, scented pink flowers, crimson in bud. Large hips follow. 7m.

'New Dawn' (6) has recurrent-flowering, flesh-pink blooms and dark, glossy leaves. 4m.

'Schoolgirl' (8) Perpetual-blooming, hybrid-tea type rose with apricot flowers. 3m.

CLEMATIS

An immensely varied group, all of which need their roots shaded to thrive. Plant the root ball 5cm deeper than the soil level in the pot to protect against wilt, and tie stems to wall support (see pages 96–97).

LARGE-FLOWERED HYBRIDS

'Marie Boisselot' (12) bearing very large white flowers with yellow anthers from June to September. 3–4m.

'Nelly Moser' (14) gives a prolific display of pale mauve flowers with a deeper bar from May–June and August–September. 3–4m.

'Perle d'Azur' (15) bears azure blue blooms from July–September. 3–4m.

'Ville de Lyon' (13) with carmine flowers and yellow anthers June–August. Avoid a hot dry position as it needs moisture to prevent early discoloration of the leaves. 3–4m.

See also *C.* 'Jackmanii Superba' on p. 36 and *C.* 'Madame Grangé' on p. 96.

CLEMATIS SPECIES

C. alpina (16) Early spring-flowering, blue in the type, though there is a purplish-pink (**'Ruby'**) and a double white cultivar (**'White Moth'**). 3m.

C. macropetala (17) blooms April–May. The type form, shown here, is blue and looks at its prettiest beside the pink cultivar **'Markham's Pink'**. 3m.

C. montana rubens (18) flowers in May, growing to 10m. The white form, *C. montana*, is equally rampant.

C.m. **'Tetrarose'** is less vigorous and bears rosy-lilac flowers and bronzed foliage.

C. viticella blooms in July–September. Its deepest purple form is **'Royal Velours'** (19). The creamy **'Alba Luxurians'** is shown on p. 104. **'Rubra'** with wine-red flowers, and the double violet **'Purpurea Plena Elegans'** are equally good. 3m.

C. tangutica and *C. orientalis* are shown on p. 56. *C. balearica* on p. 63.

ORNAMENTAL OR FRUITING VINES

Vitis **'Brant'** (20) Vigorous vine producing clusters of sweet black grapes. Red and gold leaf colour in autumn. Give wall support. Up to 9m.

Vitis coignetiae (22) Rampant, ornamental vine with big leaves, turning crimson in autumn in the best forms. Give it plenty of space for it will cover a high house wall or climb to the top of a tree. Ultimately up to 23m.

Vitis vinifera **'Purpurea'** (21) The black grapes of this vine are inedible and it is grown only for its foliage. The new olive green leaves turn dark red, then purple. 4m.

MISCELLANEOUS CLIMBERS

Celastrus orbiculatus (25) Very rapid twiner which should be bought in its hermaphrodite and fruiting form. Otherwise both male and female plants are necessary for the latter to fruit, a disadvantage since the plant takes up much room. The leaves yellow in autumn, when the brown capsules split to show scarlet and gold seed valves. Give it support. 10m.

Solanum crispum **'Glasnevin'** semi-E: ○ (26) Lanky but rapid grower with semi-evergreen leaves and violet flowers with a yellow staminal beak, borne in clusters July–September. Give firm support against a wall. 5m.

Wisteria sinensis ○ Can be grown free-standing, over a tree or on supports on a wall. Very vigorous grower with mauve flowers (23) in May. White (24) and pink forms are obtainable also, and there is a double purple variety called **'Black Dragon'**. The flowering racemes are about 25cm long. *W. floribunda* **'Macrobotrys'**, illustrated on p. 104, produces racemes up to 1m long. 15m.

Evergreens

It is a cardinal rule that evergreens should form the backbone of a garden, and this is especially true in a courtyard or terrace. These are the plants that will keep the garden looking clothed in winter in a northern climate and if they are neglected here, particularly, you will be looking out at a bare area of masonry near the house for half the year.

The best possible use of evergreens is to place them with a view to their collective appearance when all else has withered around them in winter. Don't bunch them all together but space them out around the boundaries, in the corners, near the house and at the furthest point from the house. In this way, you can ensure that the terrace looks dressed even in the bleakest months. Vary the type of evergreens, too; choose small as well as tall subjects, conifers but also broad-leafed shrubs, and both delicate and bold-foliaged plants. Supplement the list with evergreen climbers (page 20), with evergreens from GOLD AND BRIGHT GREEN PLANTS (pages 28–29) and those plants which have been marked with an E throughout the book.

PROSTRATE AND SHORT EVERGREENS

Dryas octopetala E (1) Mat-forming shrub with oak-like leaves, shining green above, and white, yellow-centred flowers in early summer. 10cm × 37cm.

× Fatshedera lizei E (2) Shade-tolerant, glossy-leaved plant which is a cross between ***Fatsia japonica*** (p. 27) and ivy. Lax-growing stems make spreading, prostrate ground-cover or can be tied to supports to form a shrub up to 2m.

Iberis commutatum E (3) Vigorous, spreading dark green mats covered with milk-white flowers in spring. (See also *I. semper-virens* 'Snowflake' shown on p. 71.) 15cm × 60cm.

Iris foetidissima **'Variegata'** E (4) An evergreen iris which is tolerant of dry shade and also sun, though it will retain its cream stripes most distinctly in a cooler position. Not as free-flowering as the type form shown on p. 38. 45cm × 40cm.

Mossy saxifrage E: ◑ (5) Pretty, accommodating, enthusiastic carpeters for semi-shade where they will prefer moist soil but endure dry; **'Triumph'**, shown here, has blood-red flowers in late spring. **'Gaiety'** is rose pink; **'Pearly King'** is white. 15cm × 45cm +.

LARGE, BACKGROUND EVERGREENS

Azara microphylla E (6) A wall shrub or small tree with fanning branches of minute dark green leaves. It bears tiny, yellow, vanilla-scented flowers in early spring. It is the hardiest of the azaras, but has a variegated form which is more tender. 4m.

Choisya ternata E (7) A shrub with shining, dark green leaves and fragrant, small white flowers in clusters in late spring and sometimes autumn too. Sun or shade. Give wall shelter in very cold or draughty areas. Spreading growth. 2m × 3m.

Laurel (*Prunus laurocerasus*) E (8) Shade-tolerant shrub with white erect flowers in spring and glossy bright green leaves. Will reach 6m if free-growing but can be clipped hard to form a screen against an eyesore. Its most distinctive form is **'Otto Luyken'** (shown in Garden 8), which has a low domed habit and narrow leaves.

Lonicera nitida E (9) Tiny darkest green leaves on a shrub much used for hedging, though it needs cutting up to four times a year as a hedge. Grow at 30cm intervals to form a barrier. The yellow-leafed cultivar **'Baggeson's Gold'** makes an excellent specimen in part-shade. 1·5m.

CONIFERS

Abies koreana E (10) Compact fir with leaves which are dark green above and white beneath. 6cm violet-deep blue cones are freely produced even on young trees. 2m.

Juniperus × media **'Pfitzerana'** E (11) Wide-spreading shrub with strong, ascending branches. Very popular and much used to give pronounced, horizontal effects to a design; also useful for its ground-covering, weed-smothering capacity. There is a golden form (**'Pfitzerana Aurea'**), a grey-green form (**'Pfitzerana Glauca'**), and a smaller form (**'Compacta'**) for those who do not have room for the 2m × 4m type plant.

Pinus mugo pumilio E (12) Stiff, deep green needles and very small cones on a dense, bushy shrub with spreading habit. Good on poor, limy soils. Slow to 1·5m × 3m.

Pinus parviflora E (13) The Japanese White Pine of the Willow Tree pattern. Bluish-green leaves and 5cm barrel cones on a pine which is vigorous when young. 8m.

Taxus baccata E (14) The yew is an immensely adaptable tree, used greatly for hedges (page 90), for topiary (pages 102–103) or as a specimen. A free-growing yew would be too large and funereal for a terrace, but in a formal setting, several clipped into a neat shape could be suitable. Sun or shade. Size according to pruning.

FINE-FLOWERED EVERGREENS

Camellias E:LH:◗ are a first choice for soil which is neutral to acid. There are two main hardy varieties, *C. japonica* and *C. williamsii*; the former retains dead flowers, the latter drops them. **'Donation'** (15) is the most popular cultivar of the **C. williamsii** group, a vigorous, erectly-branched bush, with the glossy leaves common to all camellias. Its flowers are soft pink with deeper veins, produced February–May. 4m. See also p. 60 and p. 63.

Ceanothus E:○ in variety. An invaluable (mainly evergreen) group. **'Delight'** (16) has rich blue, scented panicles of flowers in late spring, on an erect, fairly hardy bush. **'Cascade'** is a more tender cultivar with arching growth. *C. impressus* **'Puget's Blue'** is amongst the best for warmer areas. Autumn-flowering varieties include the tender **'Burkwoodii'** and **'Autumnal Blue'**, which is one of the hardiest. Full sun and good drainage essential. Wall shelter is important, except in warm areas. 4m.

Cistus E:○ Floriferous, June/July-flowering shrubs for light, dry soil and full sun. Many are tender, but **'Silver Pink'** (17) is hardy, with silvery, flesh-pink flowers and deep grey-green leaves. 1m. (See also pages 39 and 60.)

Hebe E A group of New Zealand shrubs the finest of which are unfortunately rather tender. The illustration shows *Hebe* **'La Séduisante'** (18) with dark, glossy leaves and purplish-red flower spikes from late summer to autumn; 1·5m. It is a hybrid of *H. speciosa*, like the following fine cultivars; **'Alicia Amherst'** (purple-blue), **'Purple Queen'** and the magenta-crimson **'Simon Delaux'**. *H. hulkeana* has very long mauve-blue flower panicles in May–June. Hardier varieties include the bronze-leafed, violet-flowered **'Mrs. Winder'**, the violet and white **'Margery Fish'** and the bright pink **'Great Orme'**. 1–1·5m. See also p. 93.

Rhododendrons and azaleas E:LH:◗ provide a vast and magnificent variety of flowering evergreens, though only for acid soil. The small cultivars are of most general use on a terrace, but nearly all demand part shade. *R.* **'Elizabeth'** (19) with rich red trumpet flowers in spring is shown here; 1m × 1·5m. (See also p. 60 and p. 71.)

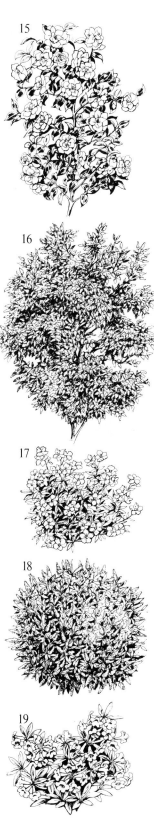

23

Paving Creepers

Whether a terrace is laid with paving slabs, bricks, cobbles, gravels or any other type of hard material, it will look bleak unless this unrelieved ground surface is mellowed with small or prostrate plants. They are particularly useful for breaking up the rigid appearance of square or rectangular paving which is so often laid with monotonous regularity. A few of these little plants don't mind being walked on (especially thymes), but for the most part they are best inserted around the main areas of traffic. Their actual planting presents a problem if the masonry has been set in solid cement; in this case, all you can do is force out chunks of the mortar with a crowbar, replace it with earth and then insert the plants most tolerant of poor, arid conditions and keep them fed and watered until they have rooted down. If, however, you have laid the stoneware underfoot as suggested on p. 16, it will be simple to plant in the pockets of soil surrounding the slabs etc. The plants will have to be kept well watered until the roots have made a home for themselves.

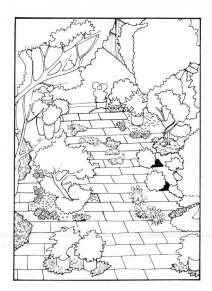

MATS, MOUNDS AND ROSETTES

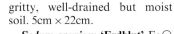

Arabis blepharophylla E (1) Bearing a mass of deep rose flowers in spring, the plant makes a neat little hummock for sun or semi-shade. The white-flowered *A. alpina* and the pink *A. rosea* 'Grandiflora' are rather less compact. *A. caucasica* 'Plena' is a good double white for sun, and *A. albida* 'Variegata' has white flowers and the bonus of cream-margined leaves. 10cm × 25cm.

Arenaria balearica E:● (2) Demands a shady position and a moist, cool root-run. Here it will form spreading mats. 2cm × 45cm. There is a very pretty golden-foliaged variety called *A. caespitosa* 'Aurea' (syn. *Sagina glabra* 'Aurea') which is less spreading.

Saxifraga aizoon E:○ or ◑ (3) The Encrusted or Silver Saxifrages make hard mounds, bearing white (also pink or creamy-yellow) flower sprays in late spring or early summer. Good drainage is essential and full sun necessary to all except the greener-leaved, large-rosetted varieties which prefer part-shade. 10–20cm.

Saxifraga 'Jenkinsae' E:○ (4) Vigorous, hummocky plant, massed with bright pink flowers in spring. It prefers sun and gritty, well-drained but moist soil. 5cm × 22cm.

Sedum spurium 'Erdblut' E:○ (5) Forms quick-growing carpets of green rosettes with rich red sprays of flowers in summer. 10cm × 50cm. Nearly all sedums are ideal for hot, dry positions in full sun and for enlivening paving, paths, steps and walls. As a foliage plant for this position, *S. spathulifolium* 'Purpureum' with mealy, purple leaves (also gold flowers in summer) is one of the best. 15cm × 40cm.

Sempervivum arachnoideum 'Laggeri' E:○ (6) One of the most delicately formed of the houseleeks, with silver cobwebs on its small rosettes and pink flowers in summer. 10cm × 15cm. 'Commander Hay' is shown on p. 39. Sempervivums endure hot, dry conditions and are ideal crevice fillers in sun.

Thrift (Armeria maritima) E:○ The form 'Vindictive' (7) bears rich, rosy flowers in summer above a vigorous, easy, spreading, grassy cushion. 10cm × 30cm. There is also a white form 'Alba' and the reddish 'Düsseldorf Pride'. *A. caespitosa* is smaller and neater growing.

Thymus serpyllum 'Coccineus' E (8) Red flowers in summer above a carpet of tiny, scented leaves. Other excellent varieties for paving are 'Doone Valley' with gold-splashed foliage and *T.*

lanuginosus with very woolly grey mats sprinkled with lilac-pink flowers in summer. 5cm × 30cm + .

PAVING PLANTS WITH SHOWY FLOWERS

Campanula poscharskyana E (9) Vigorous as a weed, which is fine for paving cracks. Blue, starry flowers all summer and autumn in sun or shade above spreading mats. 12cm × 60cm.

Dianthus deltoides E:○ (10) The Maiden Pink forms a wide evergreen mat with crimson (or white or coral) flowers in summer. The white or blush-flowered *D. arenarius* with grassy grey leaves and *D. gratianopolitanus* shown on p. 39 are also ideal. 20cm × 45cm.

Helianthemum 'Sudbury Gem' E:○ (11) Grey-green foliage and intense rose flowers with an orange centre on a vigorous, spreading plant. White, pink, yellow, wine cultivars are all obtainable, some with double flowers (see p. 39). Blooms throughout the summer, though the individual blossoms of the double-flowered varieties last longest. Tolerates drought. 20cm × 40cm.

Phlox subulata 'Oakington Blue Eyes' E (12) Vigorous, mat-forming plant sheeted with blue flowers in spring. White, pink, crimson, lavender and violet-flowered cultivars are also obtainable. 10cm and spread varies 20–45cm.

Saponaria ocymoides Semi-E (13) Very vigorous, spreading or trailing mat of small green leaves with showers of pink flowers in summer. 15cm × 60cm.

Veronica prostrata (syn. *rupestris*) E (14) Very vigorous, spreading or trailing mat-forming plant (ideal for steps) with rich blue flower spires in early summer. 10cm × 30cm.

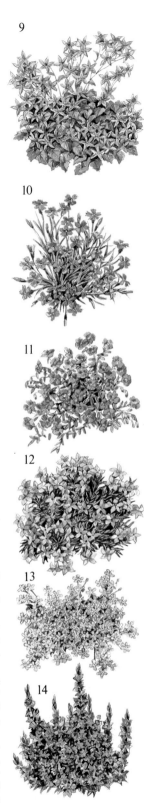

SELECTED GREY AND SILVER FOLIAGE PLANTS

Acaena 'Blue Haze' E (15) Very spreading, grey-leaved, red-stemmed plant for poor, dry soils. 8cm. *A. adscendens* is an even more rampant sprawler over paving. 12cm × 90cm.

Antennaria dioica 'Rosea' E (16) Another mat-former with fluffy pink flower-heads in early summer and grey-green, silver-edged leaves. 12cm × 60cm. *A.d.* 'Aprica' bears white flowers.

Artemisia schmidtii 'Nana' ○ (17) A flat cushion of a plant with filigree silver leaves and grey flowers in summer. Needs full sun and not always winter hardy. 8cm × 30cm.

Cerastium tomentosum 'Silver Carpet' E (18) Small white flowers on thin stems in summer over grey-leaved mats. Desperately invasive and needs confining or can be used as a last resort where little else will grow or is grown. 15cm × indefinite spread.

Othonopsis cheirifolia E:○ (19) Fleshy, grey, erectly held leaves on a plant with a trailing habit. Good for sunny steps. Yellow daisy flowers in summer. 30cm.

Raoulia australis E:○ (20) Forms a tight, prostrate silver mat with fluffy pale yellow flowers in summer. Must have sun and light, sandy, well-drained soil. 4cm × 40cm.

Tanacetum densum 'Amanum' (syn. *Chrysanthemum haradjanii*) E (21) Most beautiful mats of feathery, silver foliage. Small yellow flowers in summer. 12cm × 40cm.

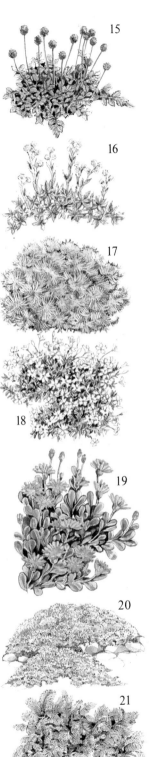

Architectural Plants

Bold-leafed plants are of great architectural value and provide points of reference in an otherwise fussy background. They have the advantage of standing out against stones underfoot, looming walls and perhaps the back of a house too, against an environment which would dominate nearly all other kinds of plants. For these reasons, contrive to include in a terrace those flowers and shrubs which are striking in leaf or habit for a good proportion of the year. Evergreens are the most useful of these, for they have a continuous part to play; but herbaceous plants with a definite outline to their foliage are equally valuable, partly because their presence (and absence) in different seasons changes the appearance of the scene.

A terrace which contains a high proportion of such plants will look shapely, and not simply a collection of oddments. However, the plants should be kept in scale with their surroundings. Some of the bigger shrubs on the opposite page would overwhelm a small yard.

SHORT PLANTS

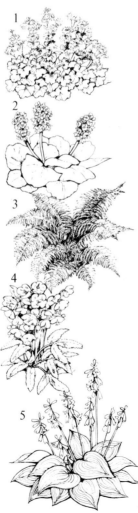

Alchemilla mollis (1) Lime-yellow flower-sprays in summer over a mound of leaves. 45cm × 40cm.

Bergenia cordifolia E (2) Glossy, evergreen leaves and magenta flowers in spring. *B.c.* **'Purpurea'** has leaves which turn purple-red in winter. Hybrids include **'Ballawley'** with rosy-red flowers; and **'Silberlicht'** with white flowers. 25cm × 30cm.

Ferns ◑ *Athyrium filix-femina* (3) is a deciduous, light green native fern. *A.f.f. plumosum* is a more feathery cultivar and *A.f.f.* **'Victoriae'** has crested ends. 70cm × 45cm. *Dryopteris borreri cristata* (80cm) is a graceful, evergreen fern with crests and a stiff, imposing habit. See also pages 38, 58 and 70.

Helleborus corsicus E (4) Deeply-cut dark, evergreen leaves with icy green flowers in spring. Vigorous and tolerant of even dry shade. 60cm × 60cm. See also page 62.

Hosta sieboldiana ◑ (5) Large, blue-grey leaves and lilac flower spikes in summer. *H.s.* **'Elegans'** has bluer leaves. 90cm × 45cm. Variegated-leafed cultivars include **'Thomas Hogg'** and the finest, **'Frances Williams'**. See also page 28.

MEDIUM PLANTS

Acanthus spinosus (6) Mauve and white hooded flowers in later summer rise on stout stems above dark green, glossy leaves. 120cm × 60cm.

Crocosmia masonorum ○ (7) Arching, orange-red crests in summer above sword-like leaves. **'Citronella'** is soft yellow; **'Lucifer'** is taller and bright red; × **'Rosea'** is soft pink. Soil must not dry out. 60cm × 15cm.

Eryngium giganteum ○ (9) Self-sowing biennial with silver-blue thistles, silver bracts and spiny leaves. 1m × 30cm. *E. eburneum* E has narrow leaves and green flower heads (1·2m × 45cm); the tender *E. pandanifolium* E has long, narrow, glaucous leaves and a 3–5m flower stem of tiny green heads (both perennial).

Euphorbia wulfenii E (8) A bold, shrubby euphorbia which needs a position sheltered from buffeting winds. Dark, bluish-green leaves and lime-yellow bottle-brush heads all spring. 90cm × 150cm.

Kniphofia hybrids ○ (10) Most have grassy foliage and the best include **'Little Maid'** (60cm) with creamy poker heads late summer to autumn, and **'Bressingham Flame'** with orange-red flowers; 75cm × 30cm. *K. northiae* (E) has exotic, glaucous, broad leaves in rosettes.

TALL PLANTS

Cardoon (*Cynara cardunculus*) ○
(11) A stately silver candelabra
whose giant purple thistle-heads
in summer can be eaten in soups,
its stalks blanched and cooked.
2m × 1m.

Cordyline australis E (12) In
mild areas, this will develop into a
small tree with a bunch of green
sword-like leaves crowning each
branch and creamy flower panicles in early summer. When juvenile, forms a grassy fountain
from a central stem. Tender and
protect in winter. Ultimately 8m
where it thrives, otherwise 1·5m.

**Globe artichoke (*Cynara scoly-
mus*)** ○ (14) A shorter version of
the cardoon, whose violet thistle-
heads can be eaten before flowering in summer. 185cm × 75cm.

Onopordon arabicum ○ (15)
Magnificent silver biennial
flowering in June–July when it
reaches to 2m. *O. acanthium* is
taller at 2·5–3m × 60cm. Both
self-sow invasively and have
sharp spines on their leaves, so
may not be suitable in a garden
with children.

Trachycarpus fortunei E (13)
Slow-growing but hardy Chusan
palm with fan-shaped leaves. Will
give a sub-tropical appearance to
its surroundings. Ultimately
11m.

Yucca gloriosa E:○ (16)
Thick, grey spiky and spine-
tipped leaf-mounds topped in hot
summer by a 2m spire of cream
bell-flowers. *Y. recurvifolia* is
equally tall, but *Y. filamentosa*
with hair-like threads on its
leaves and the similar, but limp-
leaved *Y. flaccida* are smaller.

SHRUBS etc.

Fatsia japonica E:◐ (17)
Handsome, glossy dark evergreen leaves on a spreading bush
which bears creamy flower-heads
in late autumn. 2m × 2·5m.

Fig tree ○ (18) One of the best
deciduous, architectural shrubby
trees. Details are given on p. 19
where the illustration shows
habit. Here, fruit growth is
shown.

Mahonia japonica E (19)
Shade-bearing evergreen with
spiky, dark leaves and lily-of-the-
valley-scented, lemon-yellow
flowers which appear in early
spring. 1·8m × 3m.

Mahonia lomariifolia E (20)
Rather more tender than its relat-
ive and therefore better placed in
a nook between sunny walls in
cold areas. Leggy habit, each
stem crowned with dark
evergreen leaves and crests of
yellow flowers in early spring.
2·5m + .

Phormium tenax E:○ (21)
Clump-forming, sword-leafed
evergreen perennial forming a
dramatic feature. The type has
greyish-green leaves topped by a
3·5m dark red flower spike in
summer. Cultivars with purple
leaves, or with variegated leaves
ranging from cream to dark
bronze are available. (See also *P.
cookianum* on p. 71.) 2m × 1m.

Viburnum rhytidophyllum E
(22) Vigorous evergreen shrub
with wrinkled leaves, dark green
on top and grey beneath; cream
flowers in late spring followed by
red berries which turn black.
Only for very large areas, as
shrubs of both sexes must be
grouped to ensure fruit.
3m × 3·5m. *Viburnum plicatum*
'Mariesii' (23) Tiers of horizontal
branches covered in white lace-
cap flowers during early summer.
Deciduous. 2m × 2·5m.

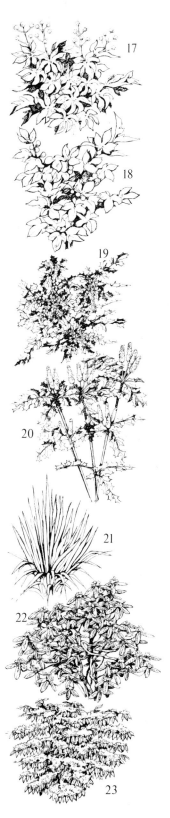

Gold and Bright Green Plants

It is in the dark and gloomy garden that a mixture of gold and light, bright green leaves comes into its own; and Garden 2 relied on this combination heavily for its colour. Golden evergreens and yellow-flowered or -fruited plants are an invaluable way of adding brightness to a dreary winter courtyard, and a gold and green terrace will give the impression of soft sunshine on a dull day at any time of the year.

Take care about the kind of flowers you introduce in this setting. Orange and yellow flowers will reinforce the illumination brilliantly. White blossom will cool the brightness. Blue flowers will always seem fresh against golden foliage; this combination is contrasting yet harmonious in a green setting, for green is a secondary colour formed by these two primaries. But never introduce flowers of mixed strong colours in a golden setting for they will simply make it garish.

HERBACEOUS PLANTS

Euphorbia polychroma (1) Lime-yellow flower heads all spring over bright green leaves which turn pinker in autumn. 45cm × 30cm.

Golden feverfew (*Chrysanthemum parthenium* 'Aureum') E: ○ (2) Golden foliage with a powerful scent when bruised. Remove white daisy flowers in summer to avoid self-sowing. 30cm × 30cm.

Hemerocallis **'Golden Chimes'** (3) Golden flowers in summer. 60cm. Other excellent yellow Day Lilies include **'Hyperion'** (100cm); **'Marion Vaughn'** (75cm); **'Cartwheels'** with great golden blooms (75cm); the green-throated **'Chartreuse Magic'** (90cm); **'Whichford'**, greenish yellow (45cm). Spread: 60cm.

Hosta fortunei **'Aurea'** ◑ (4) New leaves are rich yellow before greening. Lilac flowers in summer. **'Gold Leaf'**, a vigorous plant, and **'Gold Seer'** (needs some sun) have gold leaves for nearly the whole season. 60cm × 60cm.

Melissa officinalis **'Aurea'** ◑ (5) A lemon balm with gold-variegated, aromatic leaves. Useful herb, best in semi-shade. 60cm × 45cm.

Milium effusum **'Aureum'** ◑ (6) Bowles' Golden Grass has gold leaves, stems and flowers. Pretty with spring flowers. Self-sowing. 60cm × 30cm.

PLANTS FOR WALLS

Ivies in variety including *Hedera helix* **'Goldheart'** E (7) A neat cultivar with dark small leaves bearing a central zone of gold. **'Buttercup'** (not shown) has small primrose or pale green leaves and is slow-growing. See also *Hedera colchica* 'Dentata Variegata' (p. 20).

Fremontia californica E: ○ (8) A fast-growing semi-evergreen with cupped flowers from early summer onwards and 3-lobed leaves felted beneath with rusty down. Tender. 5m.

Humulus lupulus **'Aureus'** ○ (9) A vigorous, golden-leafed hop which grows and colours best in full sun but needs a moist though well-drained position. 4m.

Lonicera japonica **'Aureo-reticulata'** Semi-E (10) Fairly vigorous, semi-evergreen honeysuckle with a network of golden veins on its green leaves. Flowers sparsely midsummer onwards, its blooms varying from white through yellow with a purple stain. 5m.

Pyracantha atalantioides **'Aurea'** E (11) Tough, evergreen shrub for a north or east wall, massed with yellow fruits in winter. 3m. Other golden-berried varieties include **'Shawnee'** and the orange-yellow fruited *P. angustifolia* with leaves that are grey-felted beneath.

SHRUBS

Holly E *Ilex × altaclarensis* **'Golden King'** (12) has almost spineless, golden-margined leaves; it is female and will berry with a male partner, such as *I. aquifolium* **'Golden Queen'** with spiny, yellow-margined leaves. **'Ovata Aurea'** (male) is another very bright cultivar, so is the free-berrying, female **'Mme. Briot'**. 4m.

Eleagnus × ebbingei **'Gilt Edge'** E: ○ (13) Excellent tough, bushy foliage shrub with orange fruits in spring. Vigorous to 1·5m. Other cultivars include *E. pungens* **'Dicksonii'** with golden margins; and *E.p.* **'Maculata'** with a golden-centred leaf. 2·5m.

Euonymus fortunei **'Emerald 'n Gold'** E (14) Brilliant low and spreading bush, staining pink in winter; valuable ground-cover. 30cm × 45cm.

Ligustrum ovalifolium **'Aureum'** E: ○ (15) The bright Golden Privet which is at its best when hard-clipped into a compact shape to prevent gappiness at the base. 1·5m.

Sambucus nigra **'Aurea'** (16) The Golden Elder is one of the toughest of the yellow-leafed plants, making a graceful shrub or small tree. Best in sun. 4m. *S. racemosa* **'Plumosa Aurea'** (17) has, however, by far the more beautiful foliage with scarlet berries in summer after yellow flower-heads. It grows best in part-shade to avoid scorching. 3m. Moist soil for both.

Taxus baccata **'Repens Aurea'** E (18) A low-spreading yew of soft gold which will revert to greener tones if grown in heavy shade. Good ground-cover; 50cm × 100cm. Other yellow yews include **'Semperaurea'** (2m × 4m) and a slow-growing Irish Yew, **'Standishii'**, forming a slim column to about 1·2m.

Thuja plicata **'Irish Gold'** E (19) is one of the brightest forms of the Western Red Cedar. Slow-growing and not for exposed places. 2·5m. *T. occidentalis* **'Rheingold'** is broader, bushier and more pyramidal, turning copper in winter. Also slow but eventually reaches 3m.

Consider also: *Arenaria caespitosa* 'Aurea' (p. 24), *Arundinaria viridistrata* (p. 59), *Carex morrowii* 'Variegata Aurea' (p. 58), *Cornus alba* 'Spaethii' (p. 94), *Cortaderia* 'Gold Band' (p. 58), *Erica darleyensis* 'Jack H. Brummage' (p. 63), golden marjoram (p. 67), *Hakonechloa macra* 'Albo-aurea' (p. 70), *Juniperus chinensis* 'Aurea' (p. 54) and *J.* 'Pfitzerana Aurea' (p. 23), *Lonicera nitida* 'Baggeson's Gold' (p. 22), *Miscanthus sinensis* 'Zebrinus' (p. 58), *Pinus sylvestris* 'Aurea' (p. 54) and *Thymus* 'Doone Valley' (p. 24).

FOUR TREES FOR THE LARGEST COURTYARDS

Catalpa bignonioides **'Aurea'** (23) Bright copper leaves when new, turning yellow as they age and then greener later in the season. Not for exposed places. Spreading habit. 8m.

Gleditsia triacanthos **'Sunburst'** ○ (20) Bright yellow ferny leaves on spreading branches. Fast-growing but best in sheltered positions. Can be pruned in spring to keep tree smaller and induce a burst of young foliage. 16m.

Robinia pseudoacacia **'Frisia'** (21) Bright gold pinnate leaves all summer, but tinting a warmer apricot in autumn. Fast-growing and not for exposed positions. 12m.

Sorbus aria **'Chrysophylla'** (22) The Whitebeam forms a rounded head of branches. This cultivar has yellow green leaves and red fruits in autumn. Good on chalk. 12m.

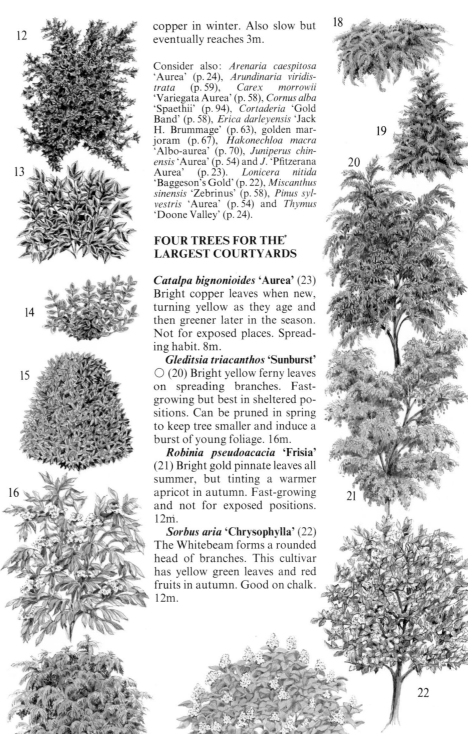

Grey and Silver Plants

Leaves in these shades act as a foil to all other colours, whether rich or pastel, primary or secondary. But a silver area or border has in its own right a shimmering effect, seen at its most brilliant against a sombre background such as a deep green or purple-leafed hedge. Here, it will glow especially at dusk, a time of day when the deeper greens of the garden have melted into the darkness.

Not all silver plants are bone hardy (many have their origins in the Mediterranean region), but they do have a practical advantage. Hailing from these hot, dry parts, most are well adapted to drought, a great boon if watering the garden in summer proves difficult.

Grow most of the plants in sun, but the very few that will tolerate shade will make a dark corner gleam with light.

The foliage of the plants shown below varies between white, silver, grey, grey-green and near-blue. The texture of the leaves is also remarkable for its variety; some are lacy, others furry or felted.

FLOWERING OR FOLIAGE PLANTS UNDER 70cm

Anaphalis triplinervis (1) Semi-everlasting flowers produced in little white clusters from July to autumn over mats of bright grey foliage. Dislikes drought. 40cm × 30cm.

Convolvulus cneorum E: ○ (2) A shrub with pale pink and white flowers in early summer and brilliant silver lanceolate leaves. Not reliably hardy and needs shelter. 60cm × 60cm.

Nepeta mussinii ○ (3) Catmint is an easy plant, much used for ground-cover and edging, with greeny-grey leaves (often eaten back to the quick by cats) and mauve-blue spikes all summer. 40cm × 30cm.

Paeonia mlokosewitschii (4) Mounds of soft grey-green leaves make this plant of foliage value but, for a brief period in early summer, its soft lemon single flowers with golden stamens give it exceptional beauty. 60cm × 60cm.

Stachys lanata (syn. *S. olympica*) E: ○ (5) Old cottage favourite with very furry silvery leaves, giving it the common name of Lamb's Ears. Pink flowers on spiky stems in summer. Self-sowing. 40cm in flower (× 30cm). **'Silver Carpet'** is a non-flowering cultivar, making good ground-cover. *S. byzantinus* is a bolder plant with larger leaves.

Achillea clypeolata E: ○ (6) Grey, woolly leaves and heads of yellow flowers in summer. Good drainage essential. 30cm × 30cm. Dwarf species include *A. ageratifolia* with silvery mat-forming rosettes; *A. argentea*, a silver hummock, and the filigree-leafed *A. umbellata*; all with white flowers.

Artemisia absinthium **'Lambrook Silver'** E: ○ (7) Bush with delicate silver-blue leaves. Spikes of creamy flowers in summer; remove these to induce fresh foliage. 50cm. *A. stelleriana* is valuable for edging and ground-cover, with nearly white chrysanthemum-like leaves. For sun or shade. 30cm × 45cm. (See also *A. arborescens* on p. 58, and *A. schmidtii* 'Nana' on p. 25)

Centaurea gymnocarpa ○ (8) Magnificent lacy, silver fronds growing from a central stem. Tenderish; warmth, good drainage and shelter essential. 60cm.

Ruta graveolens **'Jackman's Blue'** E: ○ (9) Opalescent blue-grey foliage. Remove yellow flowers in summer in order to keep the shrub compact. 70cm.

Senecio cineraria **'White Diamond'** ○ (10) Chrysanthemum-like leaves on a plant of which this is the whitest form. Not entirely hardy; give shelter and good drainage. 45cm. (See also *S. leucostachys* on p. 39.)

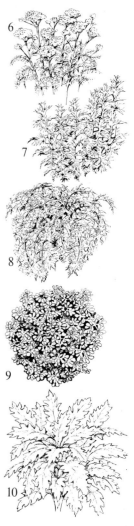

SHRUBS UP TO 1·5m

Buddleia 'Lochinch' ○ (11)
Soft grey foliage and lavender spikes of flowers in late summer on a shrub which is not quite as quick-growing or large as other buddleias. 1·5m × 2·5m.

Helichrysum splendidum E:○ (12) Felted, palest grey linear leaves on a bush with yellow everlasting flowers in summer. 1m. **_H. angustifolium_** (syn. **_serotinum_**) has narrow leaves and is more spindly but worth inclusion for its powerful scent of curry. 60cm.

Lavender 'Hidcote' E:○ (13) bears flowers of an intense violet. 45cm. **'Munstead'** lavender has mauve flowers, a compact cultivar to 60cm. Dutch lavender forms the biggest bush to 1·2m. White and pink-flowered cultivars are sometimes available. The form with the whitest foliage is called **_Lavandula lanata_** but good drainage is essential. 45cm.

Perovskia atriplicifolia ○ (14) A rather lax-growing shrub with finely cut grey leaves and lavender blue flowers late in the summer. 1m.

Salix lanata (15) A widely spreading shrub. Woolly, silver-grey leaves and upright yellow catkins in spring. 60cm × 1·2m.

Santolina incana (syn. **_chamaecyparissus_**) E:○ (16) The Cotton Lavender bears palest grey leaves on the plant which should be kept shrubby and compact by being hard-pruned in spring. Yellow button flowers in summer. 60cm.

Senecio 'Sunshine' E:○ (17) Lax-growing and very spreading shrub with silver-grey-green leaves and yellow daisy flowers in summer. Good subject for banks because of its tumbling coverage. 60cm × 1·2m.

TREES AND TALL SHRUBS

Cytisus battandieri ○ (18) The immensely vigorous and hardy Moroccan Broom with silky silvery trifoliate leaves and large golden flower heads in June, smelling like ripe pineapples. 4m × 5m.

Hippophae rhamnoides ○ (19)
Silver-grey linear leaves on a large shrub which makes one of the best supports for clematis. The female produces a mass of orange berries if a male plant is placed nearby. 5m.

Pyrus salicifolia 'Pendula' (20) Unique weeping tree with narrow silver leaves and small cream flowers in spring. 8m. weeping pear

Rosa × _alba_ 'Celestial' (21) Vigorous and healthy, June-blooming old rose forming a tall shrub of grey-green leaves. Exquisite shell-pink roses with the sweetest scent. Will tolerate half shade. 1·8m.

Sorbus aria 'Lutescens' (22) A tree which is only for very large terraces. Silver leaves in spring, turning grey-green in summer. 15m.

Consider also: _Acaena_ 'Blue Haze' (p. 25), _Antennaria dioica_ 'Rosea' (p. 25), _Anthemis cupaniana_ (p.101), _Atriplex halimus_ (p. 39), cardoon (p. 27), _Cerastium tomentosum_ 'Silver Carpet' (p. 25), _Dianthus arenarius_ (p. 25) and _D. gratianopolitanus_ (p. 39), _Festuca glauca_ (p. 34), _Geranium traversii_ 'Russell Prichard' (p. 64), globe artichoke (p. 27), _Hebe albicans_ (p. 71), and _H. pagei_ (p. 101), _Helictotrichon sempervirens_ (p. 58), _Hosta sieboldiana_ (p. 26), _Juniperus communis_ 'Hibernica' (p. 54) and _J. virginiana_ 'Skyrocket' (p. 54), _Lamium_ 'Beacon Silver' (p. 101), _Molinia caerulea_ 'Variegata' (p. 58), _Onopordon acanthium_ and _O. arabicum_ (p. 27), _Othonopsis cheirifolia_ (p. 25), pinks (p.37), _Raoulia australis_ (p. 25), _Romneya coulteri_ (p.36), _Rosa rubrifolia_ (p. 59), _Salix repens_ (p. 35), _Saxifraga aizoon_ (p. 24), _Sempervivum arachnoideum_ 'Laggeri' (p. 24), _Tanacetum densum_ 'Amanum' (p. 25), _Thymus lanuginosus_ (p. 24), verbascums (p. 75), yuccas (p. 27).

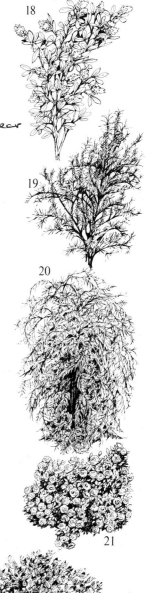

Bulbs, Corms etc

Bulbs are the ideal subject for a courtyard, because they will give colour in the minimum space and in return for minimum effort. Also they can be chosen to give flowers each month of the year, even in winter when little else is in bloom. Plant them where they will suffer the least disturbance. Most will grow in sun and prefer dry soil, but a fair proportion enjoy shade and thrive in moist conditions. Strong-growing bulbs are suitable between herbaceous plants and deciduous shrubs, even at the foot of deciduous trees if they do not demand a sunny, open position. Small, choice and difficult bulbs will probably need planting in a separate area, lest they are swamped by their ranker neighbours. Tender subjects which require a summer baking can be placed at the foot of sunny walls where they can act as a sumptuous carpet for climbers. Stiff, upright bulbs like hybrid tulips which need to be lifted each year are the best suited to formal open-ground displays. Species bulbs which will naturalise are most appealing when scattered in groups of informal appearance.

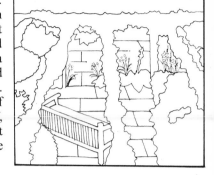

Two bulbs only are in bloom at the season in which Garden 1 is shown, but other bulbs are planted to flower throughout the year.

SPRING FLOWERS

Anemone in variety. A valuable group with varieties suitable for widely differing positions. *A. nemerosa* (1) is shade-loving with a single, white or lilac-flushed flower in the wild form, good for naturalising; though near a house, the double white form, or one of the single pale blue cultivars or lavender **'Allenii'** is more suitable. 8cm. *A. blanda* (2) is sun-loving and spreading on light soil; white, blue, pink or deep rose in the form **'Radar'**. 7cm. *A. fulgens* (3) needs full sun; brilliant scarlet with a black centre. 25cm.

Chionodoxa luciliae (4) Blue (or pink or white) stars on a bulb spreading invasively in light soil, forming mass colour. 7·5cm.

Daffodils An enormous genus ranging from refined miniatures to showy trumpet flowers. **'Cantatrice'** (8) is one of the best white trumpet daffodils (40cm), though **'Mount Hood'** surpasses it for naturalising. Of the pygmies, *Narcissus triandrus albus* (9) is shown, which will thrive (and sometimes naturalise) only in light soil. 15cm. See also *N. bulbodicum romieuxii* on p. 62.

Erythronium dens-canis **'Rose Queen'** (5) A lilac-pink form of the Dog's Tooth Violet, a bulb for leafy soil. 15cm. Hybrid erythroniums include the exquisite **'White Beauty'** (20cm), the lemon **'Kondo'** and yellow **'Pagoda'**, both with marbled leaves and both 25cm.

Fritillaria meleagris **'Aphrodite'** (6) White form of the Snake's Head Fritillary, the type plant bearing bells with a plumred chequer pattern. For moist soil, sun or light shade. 20cm. In contrast *F. imperialis* (7), the yellow or rusty-red Crown Imperial, needs sun and well-drained soil; it has a pungent smell and is one of the most distinctive bulbs one can grow. 90cm.

Leucojum aestivum (10) Flourishing in moist soil, but tolerant of sun or shade, the Snowflake is white tipped with green. **'Gravetye Giant'** is the finest form. Up to 60cm.

Tulips ○ Of the numerous hybrids, **'Queen of Sheba'** (11) is one of the richest coloured of the lily-flowering cultivars, which are fairly resistant to bad weather. 45cm. *Tulipa kaufmanniana* (12) is a vigorous species, earlier flowering than the above; 20cm. (See also p. 100.)

SUMMER FLOWERS

Allium albopilosum (syn. *A. christophii*) ○ (13) has huge lilac heads on a 40cm stem. *A. giganteum* is similar but 1·2m. *A. sphaerocephalum* has smaller, round, maroon heads (60cm). *A. beesianum* (14) is exceptional in that it flowers in late summer. See also p. 100.

Camassia quamash (15) Easy in heavy, rather moist soils, with white or blue flowers. 60cm. *C. leichtlinii* is usually slightly taller. Both have untidy leaves which die down soon after flowering.

Galtonia candicans ○ (16) Strap-like leaves and ivory, sometimes green-tipped bells on 100cm stems. For well drained but moist soil.

Gladiolus nanus ○ (17) Delicately pretty and long-flowering, peach-pink, white or orange cultivars, with contrastingly pale and dark throats. For light soil; not always hardy. 50cm.

Lilies in variety, especially *Lilium candidum* (18) the fragrant Madonna Lily, needing sun, a heavy soil and no disturbance (1·2m); and *L. martagon* (19) with pink-purple or white flowers for semi-shade and leafy soil where it will naturalise (60cm–1·2m). See also *L. henryi* and *L. regale* on p.65 and *L. 'Pink Pearl'* on p. 105.

LATE SUMMER TO AUTUMN FLOWERS

Amaryllis belladonna ○ (20) Slightly tender and needs the hottest, driest place. Pink (or white in one form) sweetly scented flowers. In cold areas, protect base in winter. 50cm.

Colchicum agrippinum (22) is the neatest in form and foliage; 7·5cm. The lilac-pink or white, single or double *C. autumnale* (23) naturalises well; 10cm. *C. speciosum* (21) (white or rose) flowers slightly later and is showiest in its hybrid **'Waterlily'** (15cm). Large leaves appear in spring.

Crinum × powellii ○ (24) Magnificent pale to deep pink or white flowers on a tall stem above spreading strap-shaped leaves. In cold areas, will do best at the foot of a hot wall where it may need watering to induce free-flowering. Protect in harsh winters. 90cm.

Nerine bowdenii ○ (25) Valuable bulb for its late, glistening pink flowers, freely produced. **'Fenwick's Variety'** is slightly taller with larger flowers. Well-drained soil. 60cm.

Schizostylis **'Mrs. Hegarty'** ○ (26) is the earlier and better of the pink forms in cold districts. 30cm. *S. coccinea* is crimson red. They need full sun and well-drained though not dry soil.

AUTUMN, WINTER, NEW-YEAR FLOWERS

Crocus in variety. *C. tomasinianus*, lavender in the type, though shown here in its deep form, **'Whitewell Purple'** (27) is a pretty though sometimes invasively self-sowing variety for winter or earliest spring. *C. chrysanthus*, especially in its rich blue forms like **'Bluebird'**, **'Blue Pearl'** or **'Zenith'** is also beautiful. 7·5cm. The winter-flowering *C. laevigatus fontaneyi* is on p. 62.

Cyclamen hederifolium (syn. *C. neapolitanum*) ◑ (28) produces its rose or white flowers in autumn above silver-marbled leaves. 8cm. *C. coum* (29) flowers from winter into early spring; there are white or magenta forms, both with plain dark green leaves. 7·5cm.

Eranthis hyemalis (30) Where happy in sun or semi-shade, the Winter Aconite will spread into a carpet of bright gold, green-ruffed flowers. 7·5cm.

Galanthus nivalis (31) The Snowdrop, shown in its double form, has many variants. A fine one is **'S. Arnott'**, a scented, large-flowered cultivar, its inner segments tinted with emerald green. 20cm.

Iris unguicularis (syn. *I. stylosa*) E: ○ (32) A winter-flowering rhizomatous perennial available in white or lavender forms of which **'Mary Barnard'** is the deepest colour. Good drainage. 30cm. The true bulbous irises include *I. danfordiae* and *I. histrio aintabensis*, shown on p. 62. *I. reticulata* is another valuable early spring flower, its hybrids varying from pale to deep blue to violet. 15cm.

Consider also: *Crocosmia masonorum* (p. 26), *Zantedeschia aethiopica* 'Crowborough' (p. 72), winter flowering bulbs (p. 62) and bulbs for the foot of hedges (p. 100).

Ground-Cover Plants

Ground-cover plants, whether shrubs or perennials, are subjects whose habit of dense growth suppresses the weeds which might grow beneath them. On a terrace, ground-cover is already present in the form of a stony surface underfoot and it follows that if you confine your plantings to weed-suppressors only around this surface, you will achieve the kind of garden that is nearly labour-free.

Almost any plant whose skirt comes right down to the ground and is evergreen (or, if herbaceous or deciduous, is nonetheless densely leafy) qualifies as a weed-suppressor. So a large number of other plants mentioned elsewhere in this book will fulfil this role and you can use these to supplement the list below of effective shrubs and perennials. However, in all cases, the ground has to be kept weed-free until the plants establish themselves, join up and take over the job themselves. After this stage your only task will be to curb by cutting back (or digging up) the more vigorous plants which threaten to ramp outside their territory.

LOW-GROWING PERENNIALS

Ajuga reptans **'Variegata'** E (1) Neat carpeter with bright blue flower spikes in late spring and showy cream and green leaves. 5cm. There are also more rampant purple-leafed cultivars, the best of which is **'Burgundy Glow'**. 10cm × 45cm.

Cornus canadensis (syn. ***Chamaepericlymenum canadense***) LH (2) Plant for sun or shade but needs peaty, lime-free soil. Creamy-white flower bracts in summer followed by clustered red berries. 15cm × 60cm.

Epimedium E: ◑ in variety. All excellent for cool, shady positions. *E. youngianum* has white flowers in the form **'Niveum'** (3), deep pink in **'Roseum'**, blooming in late spring. Other epimediums bear similarly shaped flowers in yellow, orange, red or mauve. One of the most vigorous is the yellow *E. perralderianum*. 30cm × 30cm.

Festuca glauca E (4) Spreading hummocks of blue-grey grass and sprays of small fawn flowers in early summer. May need dividing every few years. Planted closely it can be clipped or mown like a lawn. 25cm × 22cm in flower.

Waldsteinia ternata E (5) Easy plant forming an evergreen carpet in sun or shade and bearing five-petalled golden flowers in spring. 10cm × 30cm.

PERENNIALS OF SHORT TO MEDIUM GROWTH

Acanthus mollis latifolius ○ (8) Smooth, glossy rich green leaves and spikes of mauve-pink flowers in summer. Protect crowns for first two winters in cold areas. 100cm × 60cm.

Geranium in some variety. *G. endressii* (6) is one of the best, a coloniser in sun or shade, bearing a perpetual succession of pink flowers. 40cm × 30cm. Other good varieties include *G. ibericum platypetalum*, *G.* 'Johnson's Blue' (both described on p. 64) and *G. macrorrhizum* (shown on p. 70).

Polygonum bistorta **'Superbum'** (7) Vigorous and even rampant in moist soil with pink poker flower spikes in summer and sometimes autumn also, over light green leaves. 90cm × 60cm.

Rodgersia ◑ in variety. Handsome foliage plants for moist, even boggy soil. They include *R. aesculifolia* with leaves like a horse-chestnut; *R. podophylla*, a rampant plant with cut leaves; *R. pinnata* with bronzed pinnate leaves, all with creamy fluffy flowers except *R. p.* **'Superba'** which has pink blossom. *R. tabularis* (10) differs in its large circular bright green foliage. It bears white flowers in summer. 90cm × 60cm.

Tellima grandiflora E: ◑ ● (9) Clump-forming plant with hairy, scalloped leaves and spires of

Bugle

cream and green bell-flowers in late spring. The form **'Purpurea'** has bronze leaves. 60cm × 30cm.

Consider also: *Alchemilla mollis* (p. 26), bergenias (p. 26), hellebores (p. 26 and p. 62) and hostas (p. 26 and 28).

SHRUBS

Ceratostigma plumbaginoides ○ (11) A running sub-shrub with a succession of bright blue flowers in autumn when the leaves colour hotly. 15cm × 60cm. *C. willmottianum* forms a small bush. Good drainage essential. 60cm × 60cm.

Cotoneaster congesta E (12) A dense, ground-hugging evergreen mat of 3cm × 30cm which will mound itself over any obstacle. Red fruits in autumn, following minute white flowers in spring. *C. horizontalis* (p. 57) and *C. dammeri* (p. 101) especially in the form **'Coral Beauty'** are also ideal for ground-cover purposes.

Cytisus × kewensis ○ (13) Prostrate and spreading broom which is laden with sprays of creamy-yellow flowers in late spring. 22cm × 1m.

Heathers in variety: E: most LH. The dwarf *Erica* and *Calluna* are amongst the most commonly planted groups for ground cover. *Erica carnea* (14) with red, white or pink flowers and green or golden foliage is lime-tolerant (25cm); so is *E. × darleyensis* (p. 63), both flowering winter to early spring; also the spring-flowering *E. erigena* (syn. *mediterranea*). Otherwise acid, peaty soil is essential.

Hebe in some variety: E. *H. rakaiensis* (syn. *subalpina*) (15) is one of the best for this purpose, forming a small-leaved, evergreen, apple-green hummock with small white flowers in summer. 70cm × 1·2m. Good dwarf varieties include *H.* 'Carl Teschner' (see p. 71) and *H. pagei* (p. 101).

Juniperus sabina tamariscifolia E (16) Very spreading conifer

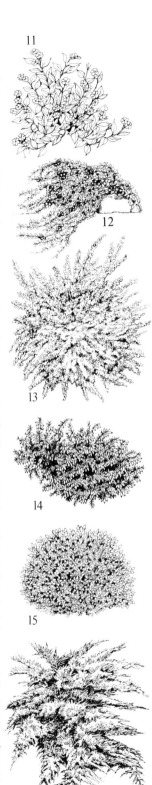

forming a flat top; foliage is grey when young but a rich green later. 1m × 2m. See also *J. × media* 'Pfitzerana' on p. 23.

Lithospermum diffusum **'Heavenly Blue'** E:LH: ○ (17) A large, small-leafed mat covered with bright blue flowers over a long period from late spring onwards. Needs good drainage and lime-free soil. 7·5cm × 60cm.

Pachysandra terminalis E:●◑ Efficient, colonising carpeter with insignificant white flower spikes in spring and lobed, bright green leaves. *P.t.* **'Variegata'** (18) has cream edges to its leaves. 22cm × 30cm.

Pernettya mucronata E:LH (19) Showy dwarf evergreen for acid soils, forming dense suckering thickets. Small white heath-like flowers in spring followed by clusters of berries from white to pink or cherry-red. Plant in groups to ensure fruiting. 60cm.

Salix repens Wide-spreading low shrub with greyish leaves, white beneath, and yellow catkins in spring on the bare branches. The form **'Argentea'** (20) has silvery leaves and makes a spectacular mound. 1m.

Sarcococca humilis E:◑ (21) Suckering shrub with glossy dark green leaves. Useful for shade and for the intensely fragrant but insignificant flowers in late winter. 70cm × 90cm.

Viburnum davidii E:◑ (22) Shrub of fine architectural form making a mound of glossy, dark green leaves. Turquoise-blue, egg-shaped fruits in autumn (following small white flowers in summer) if a small group are planted together to ensure cross-pollination. 60cm × 1·2m.

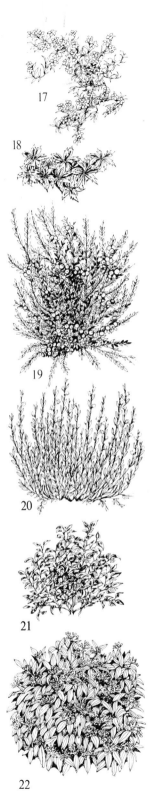

Long-Season Flowers

Many flowering plants remain in bloom for only a short period, varying from a few days to several weeks. This is acceptable when they are chosen primarily for their foliage or are planted in a garden which is spacious enough to contain many different varieties ensuring successional blossom throughout the seasons. It is less welcome on a terrace where space is at a premium. In this situation, one needs flowers which remain in beauty for a long while or are produced continuously over an extended period.

The flowers listed here are only a small though varied selection. Many of the annuals given on p. 40–41 and 74–75 are also first-rate candidates, albeit temporary occupants of a garden. See, too, PERENNIALS (p. 64–65) which includes some long-season examples, notably *Aster × frikartii*, *Centaurea dealbata* 'John Coutts', *Coreopsis verticillata*, *Geranium traversii* 'Russell Prichard', potentillas and *Salvia × superba*. Amongst the larger subjects, certain shrub roses such as 'Frau Dagmar Hastrup' (p. 60) have a long season in bloom, and their display is prolonged by their fruits.

CLIMBERS

Clematis 'Jackmanii Superba' (1) Velvety purple flowers, larger than those on the usual *×jackmanii* plant, are produced prolifically July–September. Up to 6m. See also clematis on p. 21.

Eccremocarpus scabèr ○ (3) Fast-growing plant but not reliably hardy. Little orange-red (or yellow) tubular flowers all summer till frost. Bi-pinnate leaves on stems to 4·5m. Easy from seed.

Honeysuckle: *Lonicera* 'Dropmore Scarlet' (2) produces scentless scarlet tubular flowers July to autumn. Glaucous leaves. 6m. See also honeysuckle on p. 20.

Jasminum officinale ○ (4) Small, fragrant white flowers in clusters all summer. Green or variegated leaves. Vigorous. 7m.

Roses Few climbing roses can be termed fully perpetual. The best include **'Pink Perpétue'** (5) with masses of pink flowers on a vigorous plant to 4·5m. **'Golden Showers'** has a similarly long season, bearing bright yellow semi-double flowers fading to cream; good for north walls. 3m. See also 'Mermaid' on p. 20.

SHRUBS

Hydrangea ◑ – selected varieties. Include *H. serrata acuminata* **'Grayswood'** (6), a neat shrub to 1·2m, its blue and white lace-caps changing from white to pink in summer and finally deep crimson in autumn; or **'Preziosa'** with domed pink heads ageing to claret: 1·5m. Of the mop-heads, *H. macrophylla* **'Altona'** with rosy florets has a long season; so does **'Ami Pasquier'** (see p. 61). See also *H. arborescens* 'Grandiflora' on p. 94. (See p. 61 on colour in hydrangeas.)

Lavatera olbia rosea ○ (7) Fast growing with pink flowers all summer and downy leaves. None too hardy and best in well-drained, poorish soil to stop tendency to run to leaf. 1·5m × 2m.

Potentilla fruticosa **'Elizabeth'** (8) Primrose flowers over a dense mound from late spring until frosts. 1m. **'Tangerine'** is shown on p. 93; **'Red Ace'** is the closest to red. **'Abbotswood'** is white.

Romneya coulteri ○ (9) Large white flowers with golden stamens from July on, and grey-green leaves. With the similar *R. trichocalyx*, it has produced a clone with larger flowers called **'White Cloud'**. Can invade a border. 1·5m × indefinite spread.

Roses: Floribundas ○ The Floribunda group contains some of the most floriferous and perpetual roses such as **'Escapade'** (10) with fragrant, white-centred rosy-lilac flowers. Vigorous, bushy and healthy. 1m. Floribundas were preceded by Polyantha Pompons, smaller but with continuity of bloom also; of these **'Natalie Nypels'** has semi-double pink flowers till winter. 60cm.

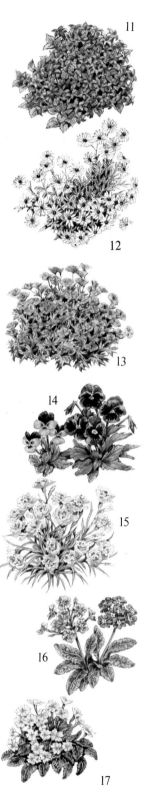

LOW-GROWING PERENNIALS

Campanula portenschlagiana (syn. *muralis*) E (11) Trailing variety with purplish blue flowers all summer. 10cm × 45cm. Some of the dwarf hybrids have an equally prolonged display like the lavender **'Birch Hybrid'** or **'Stella'**, a form of *C. poscharskyana* (see p. 23).

Dimorphotheca (syn. *Osteospermum*) *ecklonis* ○ (12) Not hardy and needs good drainage. Dark-centred, shining white flowers with mauve undersides from May until frosts. 20cm × 45cm. See also p. 101.

Geranium sanguineum ○ (13) Magenta flowers cover wide mounds of leaves from early summer till winter. Sun. 30cm × 45cm. There is also a white form called **'Album'** and a pink form, **'Lancastriense'**.

Pansies and violas (14) The former is shorter-lived but has huge colour range. *Viola cornuta* E will flower from spring until frosts, especially the white form, **'Alba'**, or the blue forms, **'Lilacina'** or **'Boughton Blue'**. Other long-flowering types include **'Bowles Black'**, the darkest; **'Irish Molly'**, lime-green and red; **'Jackanapes'**, a yellow and mahogany bloom. 12cm × 15cm.

Pinks E: ○ – selected hybrids and species. **'Doris'** (15) with its salmon-pink flowers and silvery leaves blooms all summer. 30cm. It is a cultivar of the *Dianthus allwoodii* group, short-lived but in perpetual bloom. Amongst the rock species, see *D. deltoides* (p. 25). *D. sylvestris* with silvery leaves and pink flowers (15cm) is also perpetual. Good drainage.

Polyanthus (16) Individual blooms may be spoilt by wind and rain early in the year. Wine, scarlet, pink, bronze, orange, yellow, white, blue and violet can be raised from seed. 30cm × 15cm.

Primula **'Garryarde Guinevere'** (17) with bronzed leaves and yellow-eyed lilac flowers is amongst the most distinct primrose cultivars. But there is a huge range amongst the primroses, both vivid and subtle, and

including laced petals and contrasting speckling. **Auriculas** (*P. auricula*) E should also be included, though flowering rather later in spring until June; 15cm × 15cm.

PERENNIALS UP TO 1m

Anemone hupehensis (syn. *japonica*) **'Queen Charlotte'** (18) A rich pink hybrid which is an indispensable flower for late summer till autumn. **'Louise Uhink'** is white. Both 80cm × 45cm. **'September Charm'** is soft pink and more compact. 45cm. All easy.

Aquilegia **'Snow Queen'** (19) White spurred flowers from early summer for several months if dead-headed. Big colour range among other border hybrids. Short-lived perennials, best in light soil and longest flowering in part-shade. 70cm × 30cm.

Campanula persicifolia **'Telham Beauty'** E (20) Blue cups all summer on an easy plant, though best in light soil. There is a white form, self-sowing, like the blue type plant. 100cm × 30cm. See also campanulas on p. 66 and p. 70.

Fuchsia **'Lena'** (21) Fairly hardy pink and purple cultivar in continuous bloom from summer until frosts. 60cm × 30cm. In mild districts the plants will grow large as they are shrubs; in cold districts, they will be cut to the ground each winter and live the life of herbaceous plants. See also fuchsias on p. 61 and p. 93.

Linum narbonnense ○ (22) Should be much more widely grown. Intense sky-blue flowers all summer on wiry stems. Group for a brilliant display. Best on rich, light soils. 45cm × 30cm.

Penstemon (23) Sub-shrubs for well-drained, fertile soil. Not all hardy. White, red and carmine cultivars are obtainable. **'Cherry Ripe'** and the scarlet **'Firebird'** are forms of *P. hartwegii* which flower from July till October. 60cm × 30cm.

Tradescantia virginiana (24) Three-petalled flowers all summer till frosts; white with a blue centre in the form **'Osprey'**, violet-blue in **'Isis'**, mauve-blue in **'J.C. Weguelin'**. 50cm × 40cm.

37

Plants for Difficult Spots

All gardens have troublesome areas where few plants will thrive, and these problems tend to occur in concentrated numbers near the house. The difficulty may be darkness caused by neighbouring buildings which block out the light, or it might be the sort of dry shade cast by a tree. Dankness as well as darkness is possible, perhaps in a gloomy corner where the house guttering drips. The converse of this type of problem is equally challenging where, for example, a terrace is simply an unshaded stone waste which cooks in summer. And arguably the worst problem of all is caused by a burial mound of rubble and hardcore which has been used in the construction of house or terrace. This proves to be usually a tomb for plants as well.

Short of a drastic overhaul, the most sensible way of dealing with such problem areas is to place here only those plants which will endure these particular conditions. More vulnerable plants will be doomed.

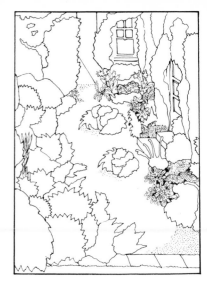

MOIST SHADE

Ferns are invaluable here, like the evergreen Hart's Tongue Fern (**Phyllitis scolopendrium**) (1) with shining green fronds. It has crested variants. 40cm × 30cm.

Gentiana asclepiadea (2) Graceful plant with Oxford blue (or white in the form **'Alba'**) tubular flowers in late summer–early autumn. Peaty soil. 60cm × 30cm.

Omphalodes verna (3) A quickly running plant with bright blue small flowers in spring. 10cm × 45cm +.

Primrose (4) In heavy soil, **Primula vulgaris** produces a succession of pale lemon flowers in early spring. 7·5cm × 15cm.

Smilacina racemosa (LH) (5) Sprays of creamy flowers in spring over arching foliage. 75cm × 30cm.

Vincas (E) make spring-flowering ground-cover, suited to banks. **V. major** (6) (45cm ×45cm) is the rampant form. **V. minor** (22cm × 30cm) has smaller leaves. Both have variegated forms. Spring flowers of blue, white or garnet.

Consider also ajuga (p. 34), astilbe (p. 64), *Astrantia carniolica* (p. 64), epimedium (p. 34), heuchera (p. 70), hosta (p. 26 and 28), *Milium effusum* 'Aureum' (p. 28), *Pachysandra terminalis* (p. 35), *Peltiphyllum peltatum* (p. 72), *Primula japonica* and *P. pulverulenta* (p. 72), pulmonaria (p. 62), *Tellima grandiflora* (p. 34), *Tiarella cordifolia* (p. 70), viola (p. 37).

DRY SHADE

Digitalis purpurea E (7) The Excelsior foxglove has most impact with 1·5m spikes; flowers of white, pink, apricot, primrose or purple. **D. lutea** is shorter with yellow flowers. **D. × mertonensis** is purplish pink; 75cm. Summer-blooming, short-lived perennials or biennials for light soil. × 30cm.

Euphorbia cyparissias (8) Stems with grey-green leaves look like squirrels' tails. Lime-yellow flower-heads in early summer. Ground-cover. 25cm × 30cm.

Iris foetidissima E (9) Broad leaves and insignificant lilac or yellow flowers in summer, showy orange-scarlet seed-pods in autumn. 45cm × 40cm. See p. 22.

Lamium galeobdolon 'Variegatum' E (10) A ground-coverer of the nettle family. Silver and dark green foliage; pale yellow flowers in early summer. Rampant. 30cm × 30cm.

Luzula sylvatica E (11) The Wood-Rush makes a dense evergreen ground-cover. The form **'Marginata'** has white edging to its leaves. Greenish-brown flower-sprays in summer. Rampant. 45cm × 45cm.

Consider also: *Alchemilla mollis* (p. 26), *Asperula odorata* (p. 101), *bergenia* (p. 26), *Euphorbia robbiae* (p. 101), *Helleborus foetidus* (p. 62), *Millium effusum* 'Aureum' (p. 28), *Polygonatum multiflorum* (p. 101), *Tellima grandiflora* (p. 34), *Tiarella cordifolia* (p. 70), vinca (this page) and *Viola labradorica* (p. 59).

FULL SUN AND DROUGHT

Atriplex halimus Semi-E (12) Useful bushy shrub with silver leaves which are ever-grey except in harsh winters. Not entirely hardy but usually re-shoots in a sheltered position. 1·5m.

Cistus × pulverulentus E: ○ (13) Compact shrub with grey-green leaves and magenta flowers produced prolifically in summer. Tenderish. 1m. Other cistus are shown or described on p. 23 and p. 60.

Helianthemum 'Mrs. Earle' E: ○ (14) Brilliant red double-flowered helianthemum, the blooms lasting longer than the single-flowered varieties. 25cm × 40cm. (See p. 25 for further details.)

Rosemary E: ○ (15) The aromatic, grey-green leafed shrub, for culinary use as well as ornamental use. Small blue flowers in spring, at their brightest in the shrub **'Severn Sea'**. There is also an erect-growing form called **'Fastigiatus'** or **'Miss Jessop's Variety'**. The ordinary rosemary (*Rosmarinus officinalis*) reaches about 1·2m.

Salvia officinalis E: ○ Best foliage forms of this shrubby sage are the purple-leafed **'Purpurescens'**; the variegated green and gold **'Icterina'** (16); **'Tricolor'** its grey-green leaves marked with white, pink and purple. Spikes of blue-purple flowers in summer. 45–60cm.

Senecio leucostachys E: ○ (17) Filigree, silvery white leaves on stems which intermesh with shrubs or a wall trellis. Small white flowers in summer. Tender. 60cm but 2m in mild winter areas.

Consider also: *Acanthus spinosus* (p. 26), agapanthus (p. 64), alliums (p. 32 & 100), armeria (p. 24), *Anthemis cupaniana* (p. 101), cerastium (p. 25), cynara (p. 27), eryngium (p. 26), *Festuca glauca* (p. 34), foeniculum (p. 67), gypsophila (p. 66), linum (p. 74), onopordon (p. 27), *Othonopsis cheirifolia* (p. 25), *Phlomis fruticosa* (p. 93), *Sisyrinchium striatum* (p. 65), thyme (p. 25 & 67), verbascum (p. 75), yucca (p. 27); also all plants on pp. 30–31 which are distinguished by the sign ○.

RUBBLY GRITTY SOIL

Dianthus gratianopolitanus E: ○ (18) The Cheddar Pink with its pink flowers and cushion of leaves is easy and usually naturalises. It bears very fragrant blooms in midsummer. 15cm × 15cm.

Iris germanica ○ (19) The Bearded Iris needs its rhizomes baked by sun. The colour range includes white, green, yellow, bronze, pink, carmine, wine, pale to deep blue, lavender to purple as well as bicolours. 70–100cm × 30cm. Early-summer blooming, though there is a group up to 60cm high, blooming a little earlier. *Iris unguicularis* (p. 33) is also excellent in this type of ground. The grassy-leaved Pacific Coast Iris hybrids used in Garden 4 need better soil and moisture as well as good drainage.

Mesembryanthemum E: ○ (20) A large family of mostly trailing succulents with rayed flowers blooming all summer in a brilliant colour range. They need sun to thrive and complete winter cover as all are tender. *M. edule* is one of the least tender. 7cm–60cm × 15cm–30cm.

Nasturtium ○ (21) Also frost-tender, but will flower summer through till frosts on gritty soil if it is not too poor. The climbing form is shown overleaf; here is the dwarf form in shades of red, yellow or orange, and with plain green or marbled green and cream leaves. Single or double flowers. 15cm × 15cm.

Sedum acre E: ○ (22) Invasive and self-sowing sedum covered with golden stars in early summer over a spreading leaf-mat. Useful in this position. See also p. 24. 7·5cm × 45cm.

Sempervivum 'Commander Hay' E: ○ (23) A cultivar with large rosy rosettes and pink flowers in summer. 20cm × 20cm. Almost all the varieties will adapt to these conditions. See also p. 24.

Valerian (*Kentranthus ruber*) (24) Maroon, rose or white flower-sprays on a plant which often naturalises in walls. Self-sowing and invasive. 45cm × 30cm.

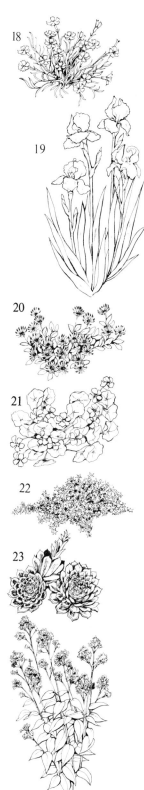

Temporary Effects: Annuals, Pots etc.

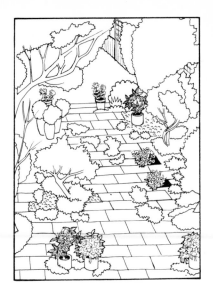

In any confined space, one needs a change of plants to avoid the monotony of looking at the same scene day after day. Annuals and half-hardy annuals are temporary residents and will give an abundance of flower and/or lushness of foliage that only the warm weather makes possible.

The most useful on a terrace are those annuals with a long season in flower and also those plants which perform well in pots and tubs. Plant annuals in pockets or areas around the terrace or sow the longer-flowering varieties in the empty spaces of any missing paving stones, so long as the soil is friable. Consider also using tender, rapid-growing climbers either to fill spaces on walls, or to festoon large shrubs or to conceal structural eyesores etc. before permanent plants have begun to cover them.

Most annuals will flourish only in full sun, but a few in the list below will thrive in the shadier courtyard, as will *Nicotiana* and *Mimulus* (both on p. 75 where another range of annuals is shown).

RAPID CLIMBERS OR TRAILERS

Cobaea scandens ○ (1) Tender perennial grown as a half-hardy annual. Purple bells or cream in the form '**Alba**'. Gives dense coverage, but needs support. May sprint to 6m in the season.

Humulus japonicus '**Variegatus**' (4) Hardy perennial, but can be grown as an annual. Leaves splashed with cream and gold. Support on a trellis or allow to scramble over bushes. 4m in a season.

Ipomoea rubro caerulea ○ (2) is the blue Morning Glory. Other forms have carmine or white flowers, or striped or variegated blooms. One form has marbled green and white leaves and can be used as a trailing plant from a container. Grown as a half-hardy annual, but blooms well only in warm summers. Support. 3m.

Nasturtium (*Tropaeolum*) (3) The climbing form flowers all summer in a range of yellows and reds. Will trail to give ground-cover or climb on a trellis, shrubs or a hedge. Hardy annual. 1·8m.

Thunbergia alata ○ (5) Thin climber with cream or orange flowers with a black centre, or white with a yellow centre in the form '**Angel Wings**'. Blooms for a long period. Support with a wire trellis or canes, or use as a trailing plant in a container. Tender perennial grown as a half-hardy annual. May reach 2·5m.

PLANTS ESPECIALLY SUITED TO POTS OR TUBS

Amaranthus caudatus (Love-lies-bleeding) (6) A distinctive hardy annual with maroon (or green in the form '**Viridis**') long flower tassels from late summer to autumn. Can self-sow. 60cm.

Begonia semperflorens (7) A fibrous-rooted begonia grown as a half-hardy annual, though a tender perennial. Colours include white, pink, scarlet or bi-colours and bronze or green foliage. Blooms all summer until frosts and will also tolerate shade. 18cm.

Castor-oil plant (*Ricinus communis*) ○ Grown as a half-hardy annual. The type has large green leaves and the form '**Zanzibariensis**' has white veins also. '**Gibsoni**' (8) has bronze foliage, small orange flower clusters. Very poisonous seeds. 1m–2·5m.

Fuchsia '**Thalia**' (9) A graceful tender fuchsia with tubular, red flowers. Very floriferous from summer through till autumn. 60cm. Good tender hybrids include '**Dollar Princess**' (frilly purple corolla and crimson sepals), '**Coachman**' (deep salmon corolla, pink sepals) and '**Powder Puff**' (white corolla and pink sepals).

Hibiscus hybrids ○ (10) Enormous, showy, crimson, pink or white saucer flowers from summer until autumn. Bushy plants varying from 60cm to 1·2m. If sown early, the shorter hybrids can

be flowered as half-hardy annuals. Otherwise, tender perennials.

TENDER PLANTS which can be stood outside during summer.

Abutilon hybrids ○ (11) Shrubby plants which can be flowered as half-hardy annuals. Beautifully veined, open bell-flowers in cream, primrose, pink, scarlet or wine shades. 1m or more.

Agave americana E:○ Succulent with a blue-grey rosette of leaves with fierce spines. *A.a.* **'Marginata'** (12) is shown here, a striking gold-variegated form. 40cm or more. Position the potted plants with caution on the terrace to avoid injury, and better omit them altogether where there are children or pets.

Busy Lizzie (*Impatiens* hybrids) (13) A valuable perennial for moist sun or shade, blooming continuously all summer. Usually single flowers in red, white, mauve, orange or pink, though there is also a rose-like, double-flowered form in the same colour range. This will not tolerate full shade. 30cm–1m.

Datura fastuosa (syn. *metel*) ○ (14) Large single or double, scented trumpets of white, violet or pale yellow on a bushy plant to 1m. Can be flowered as half-hardy annual. The white *D. arborea* and fragrant *D. suaveolens* are impressive grown as standards for big tubs. Up to 3m. All are poisonous.

Geranium (*Pelargonium*) ○ The double scarlet **'Zinc'** (15), one of the zonal pelargoniums, is the most widely grown of all outdoor summer pot-plants. Colour range of white, pink and reds, and ornamentally zoned foliage. The ivy-leafed pelargonium (*P. peltatum* hybrids) has the same colour range, but a climbing or trailing habit suited to urns and tubs. All are drought-tolerant.

Jacaranda ovalifolia (syn. *mimosaefolia*) ○ (16) Tree which can make an ornamental foliage specimen of 70cm within a season. Ferny leaves and, when large, clusters of blue-mauve flowers.

Plumbago capensis ○ (17) Lanky shrub with exquisite clusters of ice-blue flowers (or white in the form **'Alba'**) all summer. Large pot or tub required. 3m or can be pruned shorter.

LONG-SEASON FLOWERS

Antirrhinum ○ (18) Short-lived perennial best grown as a half-hardy annual. Single or double flowers in shades of yellow, orange, pink, scarlet, wine and white. 15cm–1m × 30cm.

Arctotis hybrids ○ (21) Bushy plants with daisy-flowers in shades of cream, yellow, pink or crimson. 45cm. *A. grandis* is 75cm with white or cream flowers and a central dark blue disc and reverse to its petals. Grown as half-hardy annuals. Plant 30cm apart.

Dimorphotheca (syn. *Osteospermum*) *aurantica* hybrids ○ (20) Satiny blooms in apricot, cream, lemon or white. Sow late as hardy annual or grow as half-hardy. 30cm × 25cm.

Gazania hybrids ○ (19) Blooms from June until frosts. A dark zone around the disc contrasts with the red, orange, brown, yellow, pink or cream petals. Half-hardy annual. 20–37cm × 20cm.

Godetia **'Sybil Sherwood'** (22) a soft lilac-pink growing to 37cm. Other varieties have single or double flowers in white, salmon, or carmine. Hardy annuals which are best in full sun but do quite well in part-shade. 30–60cm × 15–30cm.

Lobelia (23) Compact, spreading or trailing half-hardy annuals in shades of white, pale or dark blue, purple or crimson. Best in moist soil and will tolerate half-shade. Poisonous. 15cm × 15cm.

Petunia ○ (24) Single or double flowers in an extensive colour range, including many lurid bi-colors. Grown as a half-hardy annual, will bloom all summer till frosts. Must have full sun and very resistant to drought. 22cm × 15cm.

Sweet pea (*Lathyrus odoratus*) ○ The pink **'Gertrude Tingay'** (25) is shown, but there is a huge colour range. The tall varieties are old and often scented, though may be too untidy. Try instead untendrilled cultivars (30cm × 30cm) like Snoopea. Hardy annual.

Planting Plan of Garden 1: Small and Narrow (Page 12)

1. *Prunus subhirtella* 'Autumnalis' (p. 18)
2. *Hedera colchica* 'Dentata' (p. 20)
3. *Clematis* 'Marie Boisselot' (p. 21)
4. *Clematis* 'Madame Grangé' (p. 96)
5. *Athyrium filix-femina* (p. 26)
6. *Mahonia japonica* (p. 27)
7. *Alchemilla mollis* (p. 26)
8. *Hedera colchica* 'Dentata Variegata' (p. 20)
9. *Hydrangea serrata acuminata* 'Grayswood' (p. 36)
10. Rose 'New Dawn' (p. 20)
11. *Hebe* 'Autumn Glory' (p. 93)
12. *Hedera helix* 'Cristata' (p. 20)
13. Lavender 'Hidcote' (p. 31)
14. *Hydrangea petiolaris* (p. 57)
15. *Gladiolus nanus* (p. 32)
16. *Hosta sieboldiana* (p. 26)
17. *Allium sphaerocephalum* (p. 32)
18. *Vitis vinifera* 'Purpurea' (p. 21)
19. *Vitis* 'Brant' (p. 21)
20. *Lonicera nitida* (p. 22)
21. × *Fatshedera lizei* (p. 22)
22. *Hebe* 'La Séduisante' (p. 23)
23. *Perovskia atriplicifolia* (p. 31)
24. *Hebe* 'Mrs. Winder' (p. 23)
25. *Phlomis fruticosa* (p. 93)
26. *Ceanothus* 'Autumnal Blue' (p. 23)
27. *Abutilon* × *suntense* (p. 57)
28. *Clematis tangutica* (p. 56)
29. *Cistus* × *cyprius* (p. 60)
30. *Fatsia japonica* (p. 27)
31. *Yucca gloriosa* (p. 27)
32. *Euphorbia wulfenii* (p. 26)
33. *Bergenia* 'Silberlicht' (p. 26)
34. *Helichrysum splendidum* (p. 31)
35. *Salvia officinalis* 'Purpurescens' (p. 39)

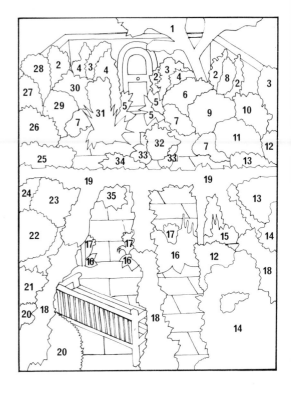

Planting Plan of Garden 2: Dark and Dank (Page 13)

1. *Celastrus orbiculatus* (p. 21)
2. *Pyracantha angustifolia* (p. 28)
3. *Lonicera* 'Dropmore Scarlet' (p. 36)
4. *Chaenomeles* 'Pink Lady' (p. 57)
5. *Clematis* 'Jackmanii Superba' (p. 36)
6. Holly (*Ilex* 'Golden King') (p. 29)
7. *Clematis macropetala* (p. 21)
8. *Pyracantha atalantioides* 'Aurea' (p. 28)
9. *Dryopteris borreri* 'Cristata' (p. 26)
10. *Millium effusum 'Aureum'* (p. 28)
11. *Omphalodes verna* (p. 38)
12. *Smilacina racemosa* (p. 38)
13. Hart's Tongue Fern (*Phyllitis scolopendrium*) (p. 38)
14. *Saxifraga fortunei* (p. 70)
15. *Gentiana asclepiadea* (p. 38)
16. Primrose (*Primula vulgaris*) (p. 38)
17. *Cotoneaster congesta* (p. 35)
18. *Hedera helix* 'Glacier' (p. 96)
19. Polyanthus (p. 37)
20. *Tellima grandiflora* (p. 34)
21. *Lonicera nitida* 'Baggeson's Gold' (p. 22)
22. *Azara microphylla* (p. 22)
23. *Clematis macropetala* 'Markham's Pink' (p. 21)
24. Holly (*Ilex* 'Golden Queen') (p. 29)
25. Rose 'Golden Showers' (p. 36)
26. *Epimedium youngianum* 'Roseum' (p. 34)
27. *Anemone hupehensis* (syn. *japonica*) 'September Charm' (p. 37)
28. *Hydrangea macrophylla* 'Mariesii' (see p. 61 for other forms of *H. macrophylla*.)
29. *Sambucus racemosa* 'Plumosa Aurea' (p. 29)
30. *Hydrangea macrophylla* 'Blue Wave' (p. 61)
31. Golden Privet (*Ligustrum ovalifolium* 'Aureum') (p. 29)
32. *Pachysandra terminalis* 'Variegata' (p. 35)
33. *Pulmonaria saccharata* (p. 62)
34. *Geranium endressii* (p. 34)
35. *Hedera helix* 'Buttercup' (p. 28)
36. *Euonymus fortunei* 'Emerald 'n Gold' (p. 29)
37. *Hosta fortunei* 'Aurea' (p. 28)
38. *Helleborus orientalis* (p. 62)
39. *Iris foetidissima* (p. 38) and *I.f.* 'Variegata' (p. 22)
40. *Thuja plicata* (p. 91)
41. *Taxus baccata* 'Repens Aurea' (p. 29)
42. *Vinca minor* 'Variegata' (p. 43)

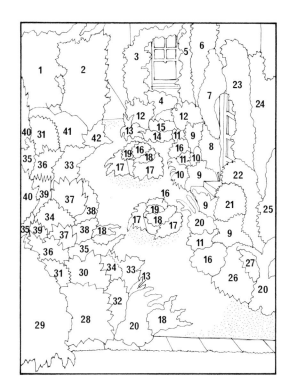

Planting Plan of Garden 3: Open Expanse of Paving (Page 14)

1. *Prunus* 'Accolade' (p. 18)
2. *Hedera colchica* 'Dentata' (p. 20)
3. *Clematis viticella* 'Alba Luxurians' (p. 21 and p. 104)
4. *Campanula poscharskyana* (p. 25)
5. Helianthemum (p. 25 and p. 39)
6. *Malus* 'Golden Hornet' (p. 19)
7. Potted white geraniums (see Pelargonium on p. 41)
8. *Centaurea gymnocarpa* (p. 30)
9. *Pinus mugo* 'Pumilio' (p. 23)
10. *Achillea clypeolata* (p. 30)
11. *Cotoneaster dammeri* (p. 101)
12. *Othonopsis cheirifolia* (p. 25)
13. *Ricinus communis* (p. 40)
14. *Pyrus salicifolia* 'Pendula' (p. 31)
15. *Hedera canariensis* 'Gloire de Marengo' (see another form of variegated ivy on p. 96)
    16. *Hippophae rhamnoides* (p. 31)
17. *Clematis* 'Nelly Moser' (p. 21)
18. Mossy saxifrage; *Saxifraga* 'Gaiety' (p. 22)
19. *Solanum crispum* 'Glasnevin' (p. 21)
20. *Jasminum officinale* (p. 36)
21. *Arbutus unedo* (p. 19)
22. *Cotoneaster microphylla* (p. 101)
23. *Phlox subulata* (p. 25)
24. *Senecio* 'Sunshine' (p. 31)
25. Godetia (p. 41)
26. *Armeria maritima* 'Alba' (p. 24)
27. *Thymus lanuginosus* (p. 24)
28. Fig 'Brown Turkey' (p. 19 and p. 27)
29. Lavender 'Munstead' (p. 31)
30. *Artemisia arborescens* (p. 30)
31. *Sempervivum* 'Commander Hay' (p. 39)
32. *Fuchsia* 'Thalia' (p. 40)
33. *Tanacetum densum* 'Amanum' (syn. *Chrysanthemum haradjani*) (p. 25)

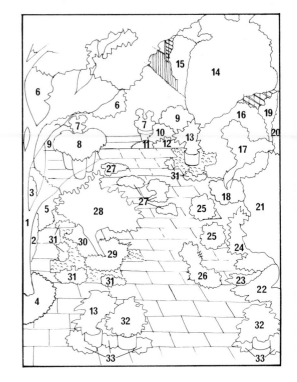

Plants for Beds and Borders

Plants for Beds and Borders

The scope for planning beds and borders is almost limitless. In theory they can be any shape or size, irregular or formal, anchored to a wall or forming islands. They can be made on the level, sunken or raised. They can be designed as specialist growing areas with imported soil – peat beds, for example, containing lime-intolerant plants in an alkaline garden. They might not look like beds at all but bear a camouflaging top layer of gravel or chippings.

As for the plants, the permutations are even greater. Even in a tiny garden, a mixed border can contain alpines, bulbs, hardy herbaceous plants, tender annuals, biennials, shrubs and, quite possibly, a tree or two. Vegetables and herbs may prove to be necessary additions.

Indeed, the term 'beds and borders' covers so many variables of shape, size and plant life, that it is easy to lose sight of the main common denominator. Beds and borders are collections of plants. To be successful, they must make a collective impact.

This is the overriding principle when composing any bed or border, whatever its dimensions and whatever its style. If the border looks as if it is simply a number of individual plants which happen to be growing in the same area of earth, it is a failure.

Other rules of design are rather more flexible and depend on the situation of the beds, on the space at your disposal and, not least, on the amount of time you are able and/or willing to spend on maintenance.

To plan a border, you therefore have to take yourself into account (whether you will weed and water as required) as well as the options your garden offers in terms of soil, space and aspect.

In the example gardens on the next three pages, different problems have required different solutions which have had as much to do with the needs and wishes of the owner as the opportunities offered by the gardens themselves. The three gardens have virtually nothing in common. The beds and borders they contain are equally dissimilar, since they are composed of different varieties of plants. But they do have the one essential common denominator that they are planned as collections of plants. In short, they are scenic. Beds and borders must form pictures; otherwise, there is no point in including them in your garden.

Garden 4

Cottage Garden

A front garden is often the only land attached to a small terraced cottage. Although the area is usually small, the owner may have to make it fulfil a number of different functions, which can be hard to accommodate attractively in a garden which is on show to the road as well as in view of the house.

The garden on the right shows how this limited space has been wasted.

1. It has been grassed over and planted simply with a ribbon rose bed beside the path.

2. Food – vegetables, herbs or fruit – cannot be grown here.

3. The garden lacks a barrier against children or dogs straying in.

4. The view is dull from the house windows, especially in winter with its uninterrupted grass to the road.

5. The road presents an equally boring viewpoint, as the lawn runs right up to the house and side walls.

Solutions

1. Apart from the path, the whole area needs to be turned into one big bed if it is to provide food as well as flowers. Planting needs to have a reasonably organised framework, however, to avoid appearing chaotic. Vegetables are grown on the right, backed by the south-west facing high wall; so is a peach tree. The ornamental garden is arranged around a framework of paths which allow access to each section for maintenance, but also to allow light and air into a big bed.

2. ORNAMENTAL HERBS (p. 67), wall-trained FRUIT TREES (p. 54) and vegetables as required make the garden functional without spoiling it.

3. A low dry-stone wall is built on the pavement side, deterring any intruders. It has been planted with the flowers shown in ROCK GARDENS AND DRY WALL GARDENS (pp. 76–77).

4. The garden will look decorative throughout the year from the house, as it is planted for colour and foliage at all seasons with a high proportion of WINTER FLOWERS (pp. 62–63).

5. BACK-OF-BORDER SHRUBS AND CLIMBERS (pp. 56–57) against the house and the side walls provide a frame for the view from the road.

The picture shows the garden in spring. Planting plan on page 78.

Garden 5

Long Back Garden

Most suburban gardens are disproportionately longer than wide and would benefit from a lay-out which acts as a corrective. Careful design is even more necessary when the garden has other oddities of shape – this one narrows as it lengthens. The existing lay-out exacerbates the trouble.

1. The awkwardness of the overall shape is revealed at one glance and long, thin, matching borders either side exaggerate the length right up to the exposed vegetable bed.
2. The borders are far too narrow to allow a wide variety of plants to be grown.
3. Most of the existing shrubs have dull leaves and are of poor value outside their flowering season.
4. The wooden fence offers useful privacy but would be better concealed. So would the coal shed.

Solutions

1. The garden can appear less elongated if a portion (e.g. the vegetable area) is screened off and the remaining space divided into two separate gardens. The narrow, shaded border on the left is replaced by a path, and the middle garden is given a deep border against the south-west facing fence on the right. Dull shrubs are removed from the garden nearest the house, but not the pretty mountain ash *Sorbus acuparia*.

2. HARDY ANNUALS, HALF-HARDY ANNUALS AND BIENNIALS (pp. 74–75) are planted in the middle garden to give successional colour from spring to autumn. Old-fashioned BORDER PERENNIALS, including less labour-saving varieties (p. 66), have ample room for full development.

3. The section nearest the house contains grasses and shrubs chosen for their value as FOLIAGE PLANTS (pp. 58–59), ensuring long-term beauty in a position which will be in view from the house throughout the year.

4. Ivies conceal the coal shed and the north-east facing fence on the left, and an evergreen honeysuckle is wired to form a doorway over the path. The south-west facing fence is concealed partly by shrubs, but also by climbers.

The picture shows the garden in summer. Planting plan on page 79.

49

Garden 6
Large, Traditional Garden

Fine gardens surround this house and back on three sides onto woodland. Assets include some mature trees (birches and larches), and a terrace, but:

1. The existing lay-out with herbaceous borders and square beds demands a high degree of upkeep.
2. The long twin borders contain labour-intensive herbaceous plants.
3. The beds by the terrace have a preponderance of time-consuming half-hardy annuals.
4. The entire lack of trees and shrubs results in a garden which is unrelated to the woodland beyond.

Solutions

1. A more informal lay-out is easier to maintain.
2. The labour-intensive borders go. Trees and bulbs are by far the easiest to maintain, but the owners opted for informal borders with mixed planting, including LABOUR-SAVING PERENNIALS (pages 64–65) and easy herbaceous and shrubby EDGE-BREAKERS (pages 70–71).
3. The beds by the house are grassed down, and the terrace is softened by distinctive conifers. They will keep the house looking dressed throughout the year.
4. A large number of trees and shrubs are included in both borders. The shrubs require minimum maintenance and give interest from early to late in the year. (See SHRUBS FOR SEASONAL DISPLAY pages 60–61.) The trees share the same virtues (see TREES FOR BEDS AND BORDERS pages 54–55), but also they vastly improve the view from the house by the variation in height and shape. They help to modify the abrupt transition between garden and woodland, culminating in the stand of graceful pines furthest from the house.

The garden is shown in autumn. Planting plan on page 80.

Planning, Making and Maintaining Beds and Borders

Types of bed or border

At one end of the scale of intensive care comes the half-hardy annual bed, usually composed of a regimented and hectically coloured assortment of lobelias, alyssum, French marigolds and scarlet salvias. At the other end of the scale is the informal tree and shrub border, the easiest of all borders to maintain. These two opposites also represent polarities of taste and, for that matter, of garden space, for the former is often to be seen in small suburban front gardens, and the latter in more expansive surroundings.

Between these two extremes comes the mixed border composed not only of both their elements, but also of those other kinds of plants suggested in the Introduction. It has virtually superseded the herbaceous border, thanks to its ease of upkeep (at any rate in its shrubby aspects), its potential to appear dressed at all times of the year and its suitability for small or large surroundings.

But other beds and borders deserve brief mention for their special identity. 1) **Peat borders** (built of peat blocks mounded to form very shallow walls with a 'cementing' compost of lime-free loam and leaf-mould plus some coarse sand) are used to grow small, choice, lime-intolerant plants. 2) **Gravel borders** (consisting of a thin – 5cm or less – layer of gravel or stone chippings above good loam) provide plants of all types with an orderly surround which keeps relatively weed-free and remains moist. Such beds also allow the choice of planting sparsely without entailing the ugliness of bare earth. 3) **Annual borders** (composed only of hardy or half-hardy annuals), though much rarer now than in the past, still have a useful role in a new garden before permanent planting has begun to form. 4) **Colour borders** 5) **rock gardens** and **dry wall gardens** (a form of raised beds) are all dealt with individually on pages 68 and 76.

Tree and shrub borders are the most useful of all in providing a visual barrier within a garden. They can be positioned to form promontories or to divide one area from another, fulfilling in an informal manner the role of a hedge or a wall. They are also ideal in the wilder areas of large gardens where they bridge the transition between woodland or ungardened landscape and the house with its more formal surrounds. They are ineffective as street barriers to front gardens unless large, dense (and possibly prickly) shrubs are chosen to deter animals and children from entering.

Pool borders are of a different order from those mentioned above in that the plants are assembled only partly as a feature in their own right and mainly as an adjunct to the pool which is of greater importance. The choice of plants also requires a little more specialist knowledge, in that there are both aquatic and marginal plants (that is, plants which grow in the water and others which grow beside it, with a degree of overlap between the two categories), for the plants will only endure a certain amount of moisture or depth of water. Also, certain plants are necessary in the pool solely for their function as oxygenators, rather than for any reason of design. For a selection of plants, see page 72.

Site

Small beds can be tucked into almost any space providing the soil is suitable, and light, air and moisture are sufficient for good plant growth. Large mixed borders, however, are another matter. The limitations of a garden may be such that only one area is remotely suitable for a border. Nevertheless, if a choice is possible, it helps to bear in mind the following factors. Firstly, that a south or west-facing site permits you to grow the greatest range of plants. Secondly, a big, deep border is far superior to one of ribbon width; 1·8m is minimum depth for less substantial plants, 3m more suitable if large shrubs are to be included. Thirdly, a wall, fence, hedge or house-backed border will provide a frame for the picture, an advantage missing in island beds which lack any such anchorage. On the other hand, island sites do give scope for beds which can be viewed from all sides (a point to be taken into account when planning their design). They also have the practical asset of reducing the need for staking, as the stems of plants are less drawn in a bed where light reaches all parts.

Design

It is best to work out the scheme on graph paper first. It will still be hard to visualise this flat plan, so you can either try a sketch or draw the plants onto a photograph of the site.

However, even this preliminary stage is impossible unless you know your plants. And this means knowing not only the colour of their flowers, but their season of bloom, their foliage, the plants' height, habit of growth and preference for soil and aspect. Given this grasp of the individual, you can then plan the whole.

In the pages that follow, plants are suggested which can be grouped in categories which are useful to consider when assembling a border (such as foliage plants, edge-breakers, winter flowers etc.). All these categories were used for the three gardens which were given as examples.

When you plan, you have to visualise not only details like the neighbouring value of two or three plants in terms of their colour and season, but also principles such as how long you want your border to remain in leaf and colour. If it is in permanent view from the house, the answer is probably throughout the year. In this case, refer also to EVERGREENS on pages 22–23.

The infinite possibilities of colour arrangement in a mixed border are suggested on pages 68–69, but the most impressive borders are always designed not just as colour set pieces but to ensure contrast of form and equally of leaf texture. Lacy foliage appears more delicate and refined against plants with entire, leathery leaves. A mass of flowery spires will be stabilised by neighbouring hummocks.

Plant in bold groups for maximum effect. Generosity of treatment is vital and five of one kind of herbaceous plant in any one spot is not too many, unless the plant is very substantial or the border unusually small. Such groups, particularly when they have a bold identity and shape, can be repeated at intervals across a border to give a dominant theme in any one season, other plants succeeding in prominence as the season wears on and changing the theme.

Fronts of beds and borders are usually filled with prostrate or low plants, but it is more arresting to allow an occasional tall and clumping plant to infiltrate these ranks. Organised variety is the ideal, not monotonous predictability.

Spacing between groups is rather more a question of experience, but certainly allow a foot over and above your spacing of the individual plants. Allow, also, regular spaces for stepping-stones, so that you can enter the bed.

Easy maintenance will depend on the amount of shrubs you can include, and also labour-saving perennials (pages 64–65) which need neither staking nor regular division and lifting. Ground-cover plants (pages 34–35) will be of some use here, too, but with the qualification that their vigour may involve you in having to control their tendency to roam.

Where plants spill over the edge onto grass and where the setting is suitably formal, it will ease the mower's lot if a line of paving is laid beside the bed, slightly below the level of the lawn.

Tree and shrub borders A border that is composed mainly of trees and large shrubs requires a slightly different approach, for very large subjects are obviously substantial enough not to need grouping. (Smaller shrubs, however, may still require to be planted in masses, if their presence is to be noticed.)

Good design in this kind of border depends greatly on form. Colour is usually a secondary factor. It is always a good plan, however, to include deliberately some late-flowering shrubs for colour (buddleias, hebes, eucryphia, hydrangeas, selected roses, caryopteris, perovskia and a further selection on page 61), as most shrubs flower earlier in the season. Autumn colouring or berrying trees and shrubs can also look wonderfully rich at a time when the other inmates are dull or decayed. But owners of spacious gardens (such as Garden 6 on page 50) are able to hold a fair balance between spring, summer and autumn display. This is the ideal, as a large border must be in a state of continuous development; fading areas have to be replaced by blossoming, expanding plants, if the border is not to become drab, and, being large, dominating the whole garden by its dowdiness.

Pools and their borders Water is of ancient use in a garden and still of enormous value, providing a year-round source of interest and mirroring the sky and its surroundings. It is rarely a natural feature, however, and for the majority of pool owners arrives only after the purchase or construction of an artificial pool, whether fibreglass or lined with butyl rubber or nylon-reinforced pvc, materials which replace nowadays the old concrete or puddled clay.

The pool is usually made so that its sides slope up in shallow shelves where bog plants can be grown, serving to hide the ugly division between liner and earth. True aquatic plants will thrive in the shallow water here; a wider range of plants will grow in the moist earth at higher levels around the pools. If, however, the liner prevents moisture reaching the pool border, this position may be dry, and water-retentive peat and leaf-mould must be added.

Bog-plants are usually associated with irregular, informal pools, but even a strictly geometric area of water with a stone edging can be improved by plants along its margin (as the illustration shows on page 73). They will soften the heaviness of masonry and give colour for a long season which is richer for its reflection in the water.

The pool border is probably a little more challenging to compose than most other borders; firstly, because it is almost always on view from all sides, secondly because it can only be composed of a relatively limited number of plants and, thirdly, not least, because the border must never be too wide for the pond which should always seem dominant. A narrow canal (as on page 73) takes only a slimmish border. Only a really large natural pond can support the full regalia of trees, shrubs and perennials around it.

No pond should have its surface cluttered with plants, otherwise the serenity it brings to a garden and its purpose as a calm mirror will be destroyed. If waterlilies are chosen, select only those whose leaf spread is moderate enough to prevent them encroaching too vigorously over a small pool. Other aquatics should be subjected to the same test.

Most of the marginals have architectural leaves and are equally attractive in or out of flower. But the finest for the purpose of concealing the join between water and earth (or liner) are those which spray over the edges to form green waterfalls themselves. Details of possible plants are given on pages 72–73.

Digging and Planting

In many areas, especially where cold winters are likely and almost always wherever the soil is heavy, you will get fewer losses if you plant in spring. The immediately preceding autumn/winter is the best time to dig the bed. Deep digging pays, though it may be a counsel of perfection to dig down to the level of twice the depth of the spade (2 spits deep). Nonetheless the bottom spit should be broken up, though no sub-soil should ever be brought into the top spit. All perennial weeds and roots must be removed, and any reappearing or newly germinating weeds in spring should be removed by hoeing or digging out or by the use of a weedkiller which does not poison the soil. For improvement of the soil, see page 16. For general notes on planting, see page 17.

Planting the tree and shrub border In this case, it is especially important to allow the subjects enough room to show their form when fully grown. Maturity, however, may be years away, and this time-lag involves enduring the sight of large, empty areas of earth, ugly enough in themselves but an actual nuisance when covered with weeds, an inevitable consequence of leaving soil uncovered.

One possibility is to fill these areas with low, herbaceous ground-cover (leaving a metre radius of bare earth around the stem of the new tree or shrub and keeping it clear for several years until its roots are truly established). Another option is to fill in with quick-growing, short-lived shrubs (such as cistus), which will give a flowery display in the meantime, but politely efface themselves in time to allow the dominant plant its rightful kingdom. A third possibility, though one which requires a hard heart and a sharp spade, is to plant up the space for fairly immediate effects with one's favourite shrubs as well as herbaceous plants; and remove (that is, kill, re-position or give away) the vast majority in the course of time when the main skeleton of the border begins to need the room in order to develop its full potential.

Planting the pool border With the modern fibreglass pool or butyl-lined construction, the simplest method is to pile soil over the shelves, heaping it in mole hills every now and then, and covering it with a layer of gravel. Plant in the hillocks. Alternatively, you can pot up the plants in openwork plastic baskets, designed especially for this purpose, and insert these in the pool where you wish, raising or perhaps lowering their level as necessary by inserting or removing a brick beneath the container. The ideal time to establish pool plants is in late spring to early summer; indeed, some (like waterlilies, pontederias or gunneras) must be planted then.

Maintenance

A border either has to be under continuous cultivation so that it is kept clean and weed-free, or else you have to find some means of keeping the weeds down if not out. Ground-cover plants, whether shrubby or herbaceous, are one way of doing this. **Mulching** in spring is another. In this case, allow the soil to lose its winter chill; at that spring stage where it is slightly warmed yet still moist, put on it (around each plant) a thick quilt – from 2·5cm to 7·5cm deep – of compost, pulverised tree bark, leaf-mould, peat or sawdust. This will also keep the soil moist for longer in the summer, reducing the need for watering. (Mulching is not, of course, used for gravel beds, where the actual chippings serve as a mulch.)

The advantage of leaf-mould, compost, pulverised tree bark and (if you can get it) straw with rotted farmyard manure is that these materials replace nutrients that have been used up by the plants or leached out of the soil. Otherwise, balanced artificial fertilisers can be used.

Staking is also a spring job, though (as a general rule) it is only necessary for plants which grow above 75cm–1m. In exposed or windy positions, it may prove essential however, for shorter plants. Brushwood, like pea-sticks, can be put around the plant so that the growing stems will be enclosed and supported by it in an unobtrusive manner. But delphiniums and other tall, very stout-stemmed flowers will have to be tied to stout stakes or canes.

Dead-heading in summer will not only keep a border looking trim, but will prolong the season by inducing the plant to produce further crops of flowers.

In autumn, the woody stems of hardy herbaceous plants should be cut back to the ground. But leave the stems on marginally tender plants, as they may be a small protection in severe winter snaps.

Before the onset of winter (certainly before the likelihood of any hard frost), all tender plants should have a protective covering of loosely packed bracken or grit or peat over the crowns. If they are tall plants, they ought to be wrapped up in a polythene or hessian blanket (ideally with loosely-packed bracken within). If slugs are likely to be a pest, put grit round the crowns in these cases too. Otherwise you can use slug pellets when new shoots emerge from the ground in the late winter or early spring.

Trees for Beds and Borders

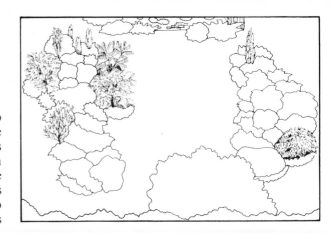

Small trees are almost always worthwhile in the shrub border where they break the bushy monotony and give extra height. Even in the large mixed or herbaceous border, they may have a part to play. One on its own can be the dominant plant around which the rest of the border is assembled. Or a number of the same species planted at even intervals will give formal regularity to the border. For this purpose the fastigiate conifers mentioned below are the most useful.

In a shrub border, consider especially the overall shape of the tree and its branch pattern, whether it is erect or spreading and how this complements its neighbours. In a mixed or herbaceous border, choose only a tree which casts comparatively thin shade, permitting light and air and rain to reach the plants around it.

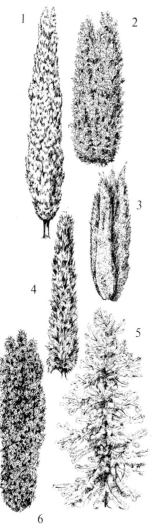

CONIFERS

Cupressus sempervirens E (1) This is the Italian Cypress which makes a thin dark column, often partnered for contrast and symbolism in the Mediterranean by the Stone Pine (*Pinus pinea*) shown on p. 19. With a possible ultimate height of 15m, it would only be suitable for the largest shrub borders.

Juniperus chinensis '**Aurea**' E: ◑ (2) Golden-foliaged column. Slow-growing and better in part-shade. 8m.

Juniperus communis '**Hibernica**' ('**Stricta**') E (3) Very narrow column of blue-grey foliage. Good for making a series of focal points or as an accent. Very slow growth but may need tying in to keep erect as it ages. 5m.

Juniperus virginiana '**Skyrocket**' E (4), a narrow pillar with blue-grey leaves, is also useful for the same purpose. 4m.

Pinus sylvestris '**Aurea**' E (5) A very slow-growing bushy form of the Scots Pine, its foliage turning golden in winter. Growth after very many years is 10m but it is sometimes included with alpines because it remains dwarf for so long.

Taxus baccata '**Fastigiata**' E (6) The Irish Yew seen in church-yards. A broad column of blackish-green leaves. 10m.

FRUIT TREES

If there is only space for one tree, you must select a self-fertile cultivar to ensure fruiting. If you can include more than one fruit tree of the same kind, you are not restricted to self-fertile cultivars, but you need to choose cultivars which will cross-pollinate to ensure a crop.

Apples (7) Apple trees are sometimes grown as free-standing cordon espaliers along the spine of a narrow border. Otherwise they make good subjects trained against either a west or an east wall. The dessert apple '**Lord Lambourne**' is a good self-fertile tree.

Apricot, nectarine or peach ○ (8) These can be bought fan-trained for growing on a south-facing wall. All cultivars are self-fertile but flower very early in spring and will need their blossoms protected against frost.

Morello Cherry (9) The acid cherry used in cooking. Good for planting on or near a north-facing wall. Self-fertile.

Pears (10) Choice dessert pears are best on a west wall. '**Conference**', however, will crop on an east wall. It is tolerably self-fertile but a superior crop will be produced if it has a cross-

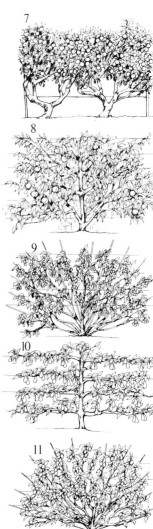

pollinating pear like **'Glou Morceau'**.

Plums (11) will crop best on a west wall, though an east is possible. **'Victoria'** and **'Marjorie's Seedling'** are both self-fertile. N.B. In all the above trees, the ultimate size is affected partly by pruning, but equally by the root-stock onto which the tree has been grafted. This will control its degree of vigour and growth. Check with your nurseryman when ordering.

DISTINCTIVE SMALL TREES

Acer pseudoplatanus **'Brilliantissimum'** (12) Slow-growing mop-head. New foliage in spring is soft salmon pink, turning to yellow-green. 5m. *A. palmatum* **'Senkaki'** is shrubbier; valuable in autumn for its gold foliage and in winter for its red young branches. 4m.

Amelanchier canadensis LH (13) Round-headed tree with white flowers in spring, richly colouring leaves in autumn. Sometimes a shrubby habit. 6m.

Cornus controversa **'Variegata'** (14) Level layers of branches. It must have room for the proper display of its tiered pattern. If not, grow as a magnificent specimen. Silver-variegated leaves. 4m.

Cornus florida rubra ○ (15) Bushy, wide-spreading tree with beautiful rosy-pink bracts surrounding its flowers in May. But performs well only in areas with reliably warm summers. 5m × 7m.

Cotoneaster frigida Semi-E (16) Useful in very large borders for its persistent red berries in autumn onwards, semi-evergreen leaf, vigour and tolerance of difficult sites, but wide-spreading and ultimately up to 8m.

Embothrium coccineum Semi-E:LH:◑ (17) Semi-evergreen shrubby tree, requiring a sheltered site, part-shade, and moist but well-drained soil. Dazzling May–June display of vermilion flowers. Hardiest variety is *E.c. lanceolatum*. 5m.

Eucalyptus niphophila E (18) Rather gaunt, reasonably hardy, slow-growing, evergreen tree with wonderfully patterned green, grey and cream bark which should not be obscured by neighbouring plants. Casts very little shade. 10m.

Genista aetnensis ○ (19) A shrub with tree-like habit. Support initially with a stake. Its green stems are almost leafless so it casts virtually no shade and is ideal for the mixed and herbaceous border. Gold flowers in July. 5m.

Magnolia salicifolia LH (20) Most beautiful mass of 12cm pure white flowers in April on the leafless branches. Willow-like leaves. Conical habit. 10m.

Prunus **'Amanogawa'** (21) Very narrow columnar habit, useful for limited spaces. Casts little shade. Semi-double, pale pink flowers in spring. 6m.

Prunus cerasifera **'Pissardii'** (22) Soft pink flowers in very early spring, new foliage ruby red, turning heavy purple later in year. 6m but sometimes clipped to a mop-head. *Prunus × blireana* is similar, but flowers later, bronzed leaf.

Rhus typhina **'Laciniata'** (23) The cut-leafed female cultivar of the popular Stag's-horn Sumach. Good autumn colour. Conical fruits persisting in winter. 2·5m.

Sorbus hupehensis (24) Very pale pink-fruited rowan with silvery glaucous leaves. Also recommended, *S. sargentiana* with scarlet fruits and *S. scalaris* with red fruits and dark leaves, both colouring very richly in autumn. 5m.

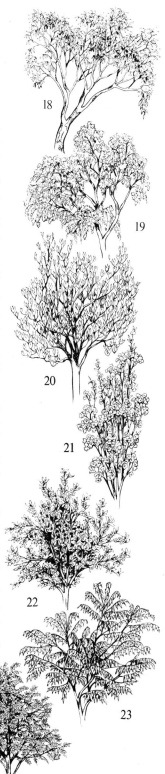

Back-of-Border Shrubs and Climbers

The back of a large border is a position best reserved for certain kinds of plants. Firstly, for the tallest, most corpulent shrubs which will act as a visual stop and a background to the plants in front. Secondly, for frost-tender or doubtfully hardy plants which will be safer if protected by a wall or fence. Thirdly, for shrubs which bloom at a cold season of the year and whose blossoms will be less vulnerable here to bad weather. Fourthly, for the kind of tall or medium-size old favourites like lilacs or buddleias, with beautiful flowers but undistinguished foliage or habit. Fifthly, for climbers or semi-scandent shrubs which need either the support of a wall or a large plant to entwine. Lastly, a high proportion of evergreens is essential here, especially if the border is much in view from the house during winter; for this group of plants, see especially pages 20, 22 and the large evergreens on pages 28–29.

TENDER SHRUBS
The following need winter protection in cold areas.

Callistemon citrinus '**Splendens**' E:○ (1) An Australian shrub with rich red-stamened flowers in summer. *C. salignus* which has pale yellow flowers is a bit hardier. Vigorous to 3m.

Clianthus puniceus Semi-E:○ (2) Gorgeous wall-shrub best trained on a wire mesh support. Semi-evergreen ferny foliage and crimson or white pendent flowers in summer. Up to 3·5m.

Desfontainea spinosa E:LH:◑ (3) Shrub with leaves like the holly, but also tubular scarlet and yellow flowers in late summer. Moist, peaty soil. Slow growth to 2m.

Sophora tetraptera E:○ (4) A graceful large shrub or small tree which must have a wall in frosty areas. Pendulous yellow flowers in early summer. 6m.

CLIMBERS
Supplement these with plants on pp. 20–21, 96–97 and 104.

Actinidia chinensis (5) Lusty twiner with hairy, red shoots and large leaves. If male and female plants are both included, the insignificant flowers will be followed by fruits after hot summers called Chinese Gooseberries. Very vigorous to 9m.

Campsis × tagliabuana '**Madame Galen**' ○ (6) A very vigorous climber which needs support. Pinnate leaves and showy trumpet flowers in late summer. Full sun. To 6m.

Clematis See also page 21. In addition, here is *C. tangutica* (7) with yellow lantern-flowers in late summer and silky,

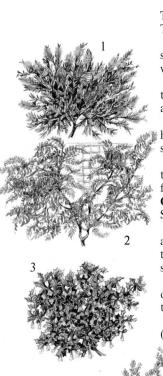

silvery seed-heads. *C. orientalis* (8) is also a late-flowering yellow variety. Both are vigorous to 5–6m.

Hydrangea petiolaris (9) Although this plant climbs with aerial roots, give it support when young. Shining leaves and white flowers in lacy corymbs in summer. Moist, leafy soil. 6m.

Passiflora caerulea Semi-E: ○ (10) The beautiful and rampant, blue and white-flowered Passion Flower, blossoming summer–autumn, when it produces orange fruits. 6m.

Schizophragma integrifolium (11) The large flower-heads of this self-clinging climber are borne in summer and surrounded by showy white bracts. Sun or part-shade, but in cooler areas it will give a better performance in the former. 12m.

Trachelospermum asiaticum E: ○ (12) A dense, self-clinging climber with evergreen leaves and creamy, fragrant, jasmine-like flowers in later summer. Needs warm wall. Rather slow. 6m.

OTHER TYPES OF BACKGROUND SHRUBS

Abutilon vitifolium ○ (13) Reasonably hardy. Mauve flowers in summer, at best in the form **'Veronica Tennant'** or in the hybrid *A. × suntense*. There is also a white form. Vigorous but not a long-lived shrub. 3m.

Buddleia davidii ○ Shrub of rapid growth with rather leggy habit. Summer-flowering in a colour range of lavender, white, purplish-red, and dark purple as shown here in the cultivar **'Black Knight'** (14), one of the best forms. 3m.

Chaenomeles in variety. Spring-blooming (red, pink or white), and best as wall-trained specimens. The illustration shows *C × superba* **'Pink Lady'** (15); 1m × 2m. See also p. 92.

Cotoneaster horizontalis (16) Attractive fish-bone habit of branching. Will lean its way up a wall. Insignificant white flowers in spring and small but showy red berries in autumn when the leaves crimson also. A form with cream-variegated leaves (**'Variegatus'**) is also obtainable. 1·5m × 2·5m.

Cytisus (tall varieties) ○ The Brooms are vigorous but often leggy plants with apricot, yellow, red, purplish or bi-coloured flowers in early summer. *C. albus* (17) is shown here. 2m. (See also p. 31.)

Escallonia **'Iveyi'** E (18) A slightly tender, but vigorous, bushy, evergreen with showy panicles of small white flowers in autumn. Shining foliage. 3m. (See also p. 90.)

Itea ilicifolia E (19) Evergreen shrub with holly-like leaves and long, ice-green, fragrant catkin-like inflorescences in summer of 30cm or more. 3m.

Lilac (*Syringa vulgaris*) ○ The cultivar shown is **'Souvenir de Louis Spaeth'** (20), but other forms of the familiar shrub have single or double, scented flowers in shades of pink, lilac-blue, white or pale yellow in early summer. Favourite plant but greedy-rooted in a border. 5m. Outstanding shorter lilacs include *S. × josiflexa* **'Bellicent'**, a Canadian hybrid with large plumes of pink flowers (3m) and *S. microphylla* **'Superba'** with domed pink flowers chiefly in spring but recurrently till autumn, and tiny leaves. 2m.

Paeonia lutea ludlowii ○ (21) Yellow flowers in early summer on a fine-foliaged, bushy shrub. Shield shoots in early spring from morning sun and frost. 2·5m.

Philadelphus (tall varieties) Cultivars bear single or double white flowers, some with a dark red staining at the base. **'Virginal'** (22) is perhaps the finest double. *P. coronarius* **'Aureus'** is unusual in its yellow new leaves, ageing to yellow-green, and best in part-shade in case of scorch. 3m. *P.* **'Manteau d'Hermine'**, at the back of the white border (p. 69) is untypically compact with creamy double flowers. 1·2m.

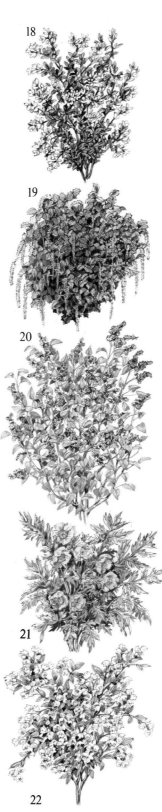

Foliage Plants

The most successful beds and borders are those with a generous proportion of fine foliage plants (regardless whether they flower or not). Flowers are in bloom for only a relatively brief period, but graceful foliage will last for a minimum of six months and will prevent a border decaying into tat late in the season.

Of the groups below, use the grasses as quiet foils which will moderate strong hues in flowers, or plant them to act as a barrier between clashing neighbours. Also position them to make an arresting vertical contrast to plants with horizontally held leaves. Put the beautiful leafed plants beside subjects of coarser appearance to throw their own refinement into relief. Plant the purple-leafed plants as a strong background contrast to pale companions, such as the variegated-leafed plants which are the more curious for having plain neighbours. Or use the purple subjects to intensify a border composed of red flowers.

GRASSES

***Carex morrowii* 'Variegata Aurea'** E (1) Clump-forming plant with green-margined, gold leaves. Brown flowers in spring. Divide to keep its leaves bright. Moist soil. 25cm × 30cm.

***Cortaderia* 'Gold Band'** E (2) Eye-catching gold and green cultivar of the ordinary Pampas Grass. Tall silver plumes in late summer. 75cm × 1m (1·6m in flower).

Helictotrichon sempervirens (syn. ***Avena candida***) E (3) Neat, vivid blue-grey clumps with arching sprays of 'oats' in early summer. 45cm × 30cm (1m in flower).

***Miscanthus sinensis* 'Zebrinus'** (4) Large clump-forming grass with gold stripes running in bands across its leaves. Buff flowers in autumn. 1·3m × 1m.

***Molinia caerulea* 'Variegata'** (5) Green and silver variegated leaves in dense tufts. Panicles of buff flowers from summer till autumn. 30cm × 30cm (40cm in flower).

Stipa gigantea E (6) Evergreen foliage with spraying appearance from which tall feathery buff plumes rise in summer. 75cm foliage (2m flowers) × 60cm.

BEAUTIFUL-LEAFED PLANTS

Artemisia arborescens semi-E: ○ (7) Exquisite silver-grey leaves of lacy texture, but on a shrub which is, alas, not completely hardy. Sun, shelter, good drainage. 70cm × 1m. ***Artemisia* 'Powis Castle'** is a similar but hardier hybrid.

Eucalyptus gunnii E: ○ (8) An Australian evergreen tree which, if kept pruned as a shrub, will continue to produce its small, round, blue juvenile leaves. Keep to 1·5m.

Ferns in variety, including *Athyrium* and *Dryopteris borreri* 'Cristata' (p. 26). ***Blechnum tabulare*** E: LH: ◑ (9) (60cm × 30cm) which is best on acid soil, has bold foliage. The most glamorous is ***Polystichum setiferum plumoso divisilobum*** E: ◑ (10), needing moist soil but good drainage. 60cm × 1m.

Ferula communis gigantea ○ (11) A towering fennel (not the culinary variety) which resembles a deep green 3m plume of smoke. Yellow flowers in summer. 1m spread.

Veratrum (12) Handsome, herbaceous plant best displayed at the border's front. Spikes of white (***V. album***), maroon (***V. nigrum***) or green (***V. viride***) flowers are produced in late summer. 90–150cm × 1m.

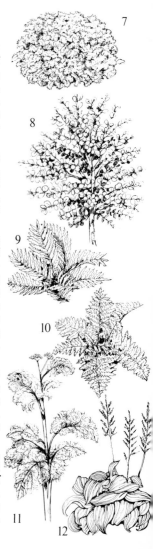

PURPLE-LEAFED PLANTS

Acer palmatum **'Dissectum Atro-purpureum'** (13) Hummocky shrub with very finely cut purple-bronze leaves reddening in the autumn. The plain green cultivar (*A.p.* **'Dissectum'**) would be well worth including in the previous column too. Slow-growing to 1·5m × 2·5m.

Berberis thunbergii **'Rose Glow'** (14) Prettiest of the purple-leaved berberis with new growth on the shrub speckled with pale and deep pink before darkening. Bushy. 1·3m.

Corylus maxima **'Atropurpurea'** (15) Very dark-leafed suckering nut. Heavy presence, but good for contrasting purposes or for emphasising a very big red border. 4·5m × 5m.

Cotinus coggyria **'Royal Purple'** (16) Very dark-foliaged shrub with feathery pink flowers in summer that resemble puffs of smoke on and around the bush. 3·5m.

Rosa rubrifolia (syn. **R. glauca**) (17) A shrub rose, and one of the most delicate subjects in this column, with mauve-grey leaves and, in midsummer, small pink, white-centred, single flowers followed by red fruits. 2m.

Sedum maximum atropur-pureum ○ (18) Bronze-purple succulent leaves on red stems with a sadly drooping habit. Pale pink flower heads in late summer to autumn. 40cm × 30cm.

Viola labradorica E (19) An invaluable spreading and self-seeding little plant (good everywhere except invading a precious rockery) with dark leaves and, in spring and early summer, pale violet scentless flowers. Happy in sun or shade. 15cm × 22cm.

VARIEGATED-LEAFED PLANTS

Aralia elata **'Variegata'** (20) Outstanding 3·5m shrub or small tree with margined-white leaves and foaming sprays of white flowers in late summer. There is also a yellow-variegated form called **'Aureovariegata'**.

Arundinaria viridistriata E: ○ (21) Striking, clump-forming bamboo with gold and green striped leaves on purple canes. 1m–2m.

Brunnera macrophylla **'Varie-gata'** ◑ (22) Eye-catching cream and green leaves (some almost entirely cream) on a herbaceous plant with blue flowers in spring. 40cm × 30cm.

Cornus alba **'Elegantissima'** (23) Useful shrub with white marked grey-green leaves. Suitable for neighbouring dark-leafed shrubs. 3m. See also *Cornus controversa* 'Variegata' on page 55.

Leucothöe fontanesiana **'Rain-bow'** E:LH: ◑ (24) Handsome evergreen shrub for acid soils with glossy, purple-green leaves bearing pink, yellow and cream variegation. Drooping sprays of white flowers in late spring. Shade. 75cm × 1m.

Symphytum peregrinum **'Vari-egatum'** E (25) The variegated comfrey which is sometimes marketed under a slightly different name. Useful herbaceous subject with dazzling cream-margined green leaves and blue-mauve flowers in high summer. 75cm × 45cm.

Weigela florida **'Variegata'** (26) An exceedingly pretty, bushy shrub the leaves of which have fine cream margins. Soft pink flowers in early summer when it is one of the most attractive plants in the garden. 2m.

Shrubs for Seasonal Display

Whether you are planting a mixed or a shrub border, try to ensure some continuity of flowering throughout the year. A selection of flowers for winter is given overleaf, but here is a choice of some of the best flowering shrubs for a spring to autumn display. They represent a possible nucleus to which you can add shrubs from the rest of the book.

You might decide to confine yourself to different representatives of just one (or two) genus for a particular season. If so, arguably the best for spring are camellias; for midsummer and after, roses (with cistus quite a good second in mild-winter areas, even though they are not reliably hardy nor as long-lived); for later summer and into autumn, hydrangeas. These groups alone will give you an enormous choice of cultivars.

SPRING

Berberis darwinii E (1) Clustered orange flowers followed by dusky blue fruits on a large, weed-suppressing shrub, growing to 3m.

Camellia E:LH:◑ in variety. (For the main differences between *C. japonica* and *C. williamsii* see p. 23.) *C.j.* **'Jupiter'** (2) is vigorous and upright with single or semi-double red flowers. ***C.w.* 'E.G. Waterhouse'** with pale pink formal double flowers is even more erect (2·5m × 1·2m) and the best for small spaces. At the other extreme, *C.j.* **'Elegans'** with rose anemone-form flowers

has such spreading growth that it serves as a weed-suppressor (1·8m × 2·25m +). See also p. 63.

Forsythia (3) Vigorous shrub which makes a very showy display early in the year, but has dull foliage. One of the best cultivars is **'Lynwood'**. 3m.

Magnolia liliflora* 'Nigra'** LH:○ (4) Dark, wine-red flowers in spring and recurrently in summer. A compact shrub to 2m. Or include ***M. stellata (not LH) with scented, white, starry flowers. Slow to 2m.

Rhododendron E:LH:◑ Two good forms are **R. 'Praecox'** (semi-E) with early rosy-purple flowers, 1·2m: and ***R. yakushimanum*** (5) with pink buds opening to white bells, and silvery new shoots in spring against deep green mature foliage. 1m × 1·2m. See also p. 23 and p. 71.

Spiraea* × *arguta (6) The most elegant of the spiraeas with arching growth, festooned with white flowers. 2m.

SUMMER

Cistus E:○ (see also p. 23 and p. 39). Beautiful but slightly tender shrubs requiring full sun, light soil and no manure. Among the best are *C.* × *cyprius* (white flowers with a deep red central blotch, growing to 2m); *C.* × *loretii* (similar flowers but growing to 60cm); the magenta pink *C.* × *pulverulentus* shown on page 39 and *C.* × *purpureus* (7) with bushy, spreading growth to 1·5m × 2m.

Paeonia suffruticosa ○ The Tree Peony is a glorious shrub. There are cultivars with double or single flowers in early summer of white, pink, red or lilac; or there are yellow hybrids. We show here **'Duchess of Marlborough'** (8). Shade from morning sun. Height range 60cm–1·5m. See also *P. lutea ludlowii* on p. 57.

Rose ○ A vast genus, but the most useful roses for the border are either the repeat-flowering shrub roses, or reasonably disease-resistant cultivars of the floribunda roses, or else a selected few of those roses that supply a fine display of autumn fruit after blooming. Of the first group we show here an old Hybrid Musk shrub rose, **'Cornelia'** (9), with clusters of small, pink, salmon-flushed flowers June-October; 1·8m × 2m. Next is **'Golden Wings'** (10), one of the most elegant of the modern shrub roses, a large single yellow in continuous bloom, growing to 1·2m. Below is a bronzed-leaved, dark red floribunda, called **'Lilli Marlene'** (11) at 75cm. And the fruiting category of roses is represented by **'Frau Dagmar Hastrup'** (12), a healthy Rugosa rose with large, single pink flowers from early to late summer, followed by crimson heps; 1·5m. See also roses on p. 36.

SUMMER TO AUTUMN

Deutzia setchuenensis corymbiflora (13) Most of the deutzias are pretty, summer-flowering shrubs, but this is arguably the most elegant and more valuable for its later blooms. Starry white flowers in corymbs. 1·5m.

Fuchsia (see also p. 37 and p. 93) Of the hardy cultivars, a few of the most useful in the border are *F. magellanica* (scarlet and violet or white), *F.m.* **'Riccartonii'** (scarlet and violet), **'Mme. Cornelissen'** (red and white) and **'Mrs. Popple'** (14). 1m.

Hydrangeas ◑ A group of shrubs making the main display after midsummer roses. Of the large and varied genus, we show *H. macrophylla* **'Ami Pasquier'** (15), a dark rose 'mophead' (1·2m); *H.m.* **'Blue Wave'** (16), a

vigorous lace-cap of 2m × 2·2m; *H. paniculata* **'Grandiflora'** (17), 2m; and lastly, *H. villosa* (18), the largest and most handsome for the back of a shady shrub border. 2·5m. See also further varieties on p. 36 and p. 94. Lime-free soil is necessary to ensure blue flowers; slightly limy soil will produce pink or red flowers; very alkaline soils are unsuitable. All are moisture-loving and are happy in part-shade.

Consider also hebes on p. 23.

AUTUMN COLOUR, BERRIES OR FRUIT

Enkianthus campanulatus LH:◑ (19) Pale buff, pendent bell-flowers in clusters in early summer, a tiered-branch habit and rich red and yellow autumn foliage make this a valuable shrub for all seasons. Peaty, lime-free soil, part-shade. 2m.

Fothergilla major (monticola) LH (20) White, bottle-brush flower-spikes in spring, flame and yellow autumn foliage. Peaty, lime-free soil. 2m.

Hypericum inodorum **'Elstead'** (21) Yellow flowers in summer producing red fruits which combine attractively with later blooms. 1m × 1·5m.

Rosa moyesii **'Geranium'** (22) Single scarlet flowers in June followed by large, red, bottle-shaped autumn fruits. Bushy, erect growth. 2·5m × 3m.

Skimmia japonica E:◑ (23) The females berry if pollinated by a male. The best combination is the female cultivar **'Foremanii'** which produces abundant berries, planted with the male **'Fragrans'** with its scented, creamy flower spikes in early summer. Both are evergreen and better in part-shade. 1m × 1·5m.

Viburnum betulifolium (24) Marvellous display of clustered, shiny, red berries weighting the branches, but only a candidate for the very big shrub border, as a group of bushes (of different clones) is needed for sure fruiting and each bush grows to 3·5m.

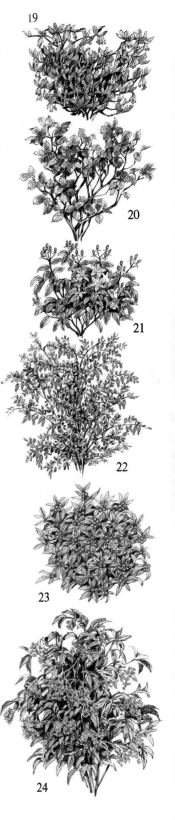

Winter Flowers

A problem common to all gardens in cold climates is how to keep them attractive and inviting throughout winter. One solution, already described (see pages 22–23), is to include a high proportion of evergreens amongst the plants. The other answer is to establish a fair number of winter-flowering subjects. Admittedly the amount of plants that bloom reliably in winter is minuscule compared with their spring and summer counterparts, but the actual range is nonetheless wide and includes bulbs, herbaceous plants, small and large shrubs. Plant the small subjects in strong clusters, spaced at intervals so that their presence can be seen at a distance and so that they enliven a greater area of the border.

Supplement the list below with the bulbs on page 33, the brightly-coloured evergreens on pages 28–29, and some of the bolder-leafed evergreens on pages 26–27. Mahonias are indispensable (shown on page 27), as are *Garrya elliptica* (page 90) and the flowering cherry called *Prunus subhirtella* 'Autumnalis', shown on page 18.

BULBS

Crocus laevigatus ○ This is a very late autumnal species blooming in November, with finely-marked silver-lavender petals. A variant called ***C.l. fontenayi*** (1) has slightly darker base colour and markings and blooms in December. 7·5cm.

Iris danfordiae ◑ (2) Sturdy little yellow iris with good weather resistance. Best in moist shade. January–February. 12·5 cm. Also shown is ***Iris histrio aintabensis*** (3) with bright blue blooms. Again, good in bad weather. February. Moist shade. 12·5cm.

Narcissus bulbodicum ○ The yellow hoop-petticoat narcissi are spring charmers, one of the earliest and best being the soft lemon-yellow ***N.b. romieuxii*** (4) in January. Good drainage essential. Sun. 12·5cm.

Scilla tubergeniana ○ (5) Each bulb produces about three flower spikes, the silver-blue petals marked with a darker blue line. Good naturaliser. February. 10cm.

HERBACEOUS PLANTS

Hellebores E: ◑ The most invaluable of all winter flowers. See *Helleborus corsicus* (p. 26), but include too **H. orientalis** (6) (February on) in a colour range from cream to deep red; also the white Christmas Rose, **H. niger**, though it is not always easy to grow. We show here the garnet-red (not E) **H. atrorubens** (from December on) and the green-flowered **H. foetidus** (7) (February on). Both 30cm × 30cm.

Hepaticas (sometimes called **Anemone hepatica**) LH: ◑ Single or double flowers, in a colour range of blue, pink or white. Here we show **Hepatica × ballardii** (8). All need peaty soil and part shade. February on. 7·5cm × 15cm.

Primula 'Wanda' (9) Single primrose with rich magenta blooms from January on. 7·5cm × 15cm.

Pulmonaria E: ◑ A varied group. The earliest is **P. rubra** (10) with coral red flowers from January on. **P. saccharata** has spotted leaves and pink and blue flowers; **P. angustifolia azurea** has intense blue flowers, both plants blooming a few weeks later. All 15–30cm × 30cm.

Viola odorata E (11) The Sweet Violet can be in bloom from February on. Wine-red, white, pink and yellow cultivars as well as violet. 10cm × 15cm.

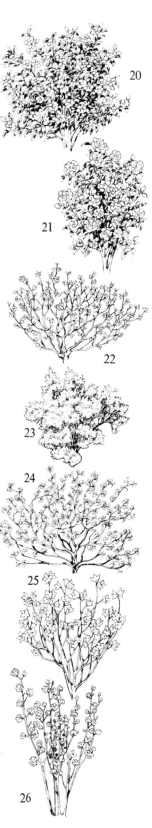

SMALLER SHRUBS

Corylopsis pauciflora LH (12) Pale yellow flowers along the branches in March. 1m.

Daphne mezereum (13) Scented reddish purple flowers (or white in the variety **'Alba'**) along the stems in February. 1·3m. Illustrated, too is the shapelier **D. odora 'Aureomarginata'** (14) with cream-bordered evergreen leaves and intensely fragrant pink flowers. Give sunny, sheltered position. 1m × 1·5m.

Erica × darleyensis E (15) A lime-tolerant hybrid flowering November–April. Usually white, pink or dark rose flowers. There is a golden-leaved cultivar called **'Jack H. Brummage'** with pink flowers. 45cm.

Grevillea rosmarinifolia E:LH: ○ (16) A tender evergreen Australian with deep rose, terminal flowers as late as November and early as March. Give sun and shelter. 1·5m.

Rhododendron moupinense E: LH:◑ (17) Species with white, pale or dark pink flowers (sometimes freckled) blooming February–March. Peaty soil and part shade. 1m.

CLIMBERS

Clematis cirrhosa balearica E (18) Give sheltered wall for flowers which appear from January onwards. Finely-cut leaves and pale green, nodding blooms with red spots within. Up to 4m.

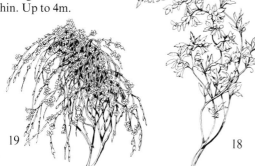

Jasminum nudiflorum (19) A shrub best trained on a wall to control its long, green, trailing stems. Wonderful show of yellow flowers. 4m × 4m +.

LARGE SHRUBS

***Camellia sasanqua* 'Narumi-gata'** E:LH:◑ (20) Carmine buds and single white flowers from November on. Needs sheltered wall position. The double white **C. japonica 'Nobilissima'** is early, too; also **C. japonica 'Gloire de Nantes'** (21) with rose-pink semi-double flowers. Eventually 3m + × 3m +. Both are best by a wall facing west or north-west.

Chimonanthus praecox ○ (22) Very fragrant pale yellow flowers, stained purple, rather larger in the cultivar **'Grandiflorus'**. Give it a sunny wall. 2·5m.

Erica canaliculata E:LH (23) is a tree-heath with white or pinkish flowers January–March and plumose foliage. Needs shelter even in mild areas as it is not reliably hardy. 1·5m +.

***Hamamelis mollis* 'Pallida'** LH (24) One of the loveliest Chinese Witch-Hazels with spreading branches massed in February onwards with pale yellow flowers. Bold leaves. 4m.

Rhododendron mucronulatum LH:◑ (25) Rather gaunt deciduous or semi-deciduous bush, but charming, pale to deep pink-purple flowers December–March. Group for effect. 2·5m.

***Viburnum × bodnantense* 'Dawn'** (26) A fast-growing hybrid with apple blossom-pink flowers November–February. The habit of growth is slim and erect. 3m.

Labour-Saving Perennials

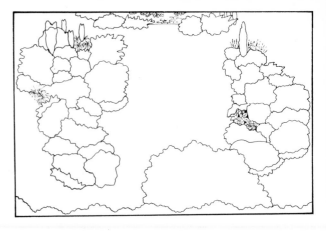

One criticism levelled at the mixed border is that it involves its owner in hard work to make it prosper. This need not be true. A mixed border is easy to maintain so long as its inmates are carefully selected with this aim in mind. Plan it along the lines suggested on page 52, and when you come to choose hardy perennials, pick them from the following list. All the plants on this page and the next have been chosen not only for their beauty but also for their labour-saving qualities. You won't need to stake them or lift and divide them regularly to keep them flourishing. If you give them the conditions they need, and mulch as required (page 53), they will thrive undisturbed in the same position for many years, and there are some which insist on being left alone for ever. Plant in sun unless otherwise stated.

Agapanthus **'Headbourne Hybrids'** ○ (1) Handsome, relatively hardy clump-forming plants bearing large heads of deep or pale blue tubular flowers in mid–late summer. 75cm. *A. campanulatus* is not so hardy, needing well-drained soil and winter protection in cold areas. Pale blue in the type, though there is also a fine white form.

Aruncus sylvester (syn. *A. dioicus*) ◑ (2) Clump-forming foliage plant with creamy plumes of starry flowers in mid-summer. Part-shade and good, moist soil. 1·2m × 1m.

Aster × frikartii ○ (3) The easiest and one of the prettiest asters with lavender-blue flowers July–October. Pink and deeper blue cultivars are also obtainable. 90cm × 60cm.

Astilbe ◑ Needs good, moist soil and part shade. There are many hybrids flowering in summer with a colour range through scarlet, pink and white. **'Fanal'** (4), the deepest red is only 40cm × 45cm. Usual height 60–90cm.

Astrantia carniolica (5) Easy, clump-forming plant in sun or shade with pin-cushion flowers surrounded by bracts. *A. maxima* has pinkish flowers with rosy bracts. Both flower for a long period in summer. 75cm × 45cm.

Centaurea dealbata **'John Coutts'** ○ (6) Pink cornflowers throughout the summer above greyish leaves. Spreading plant which needs good drainage. 60cm × 45cm.

Coreopsis verticillata ○ (7) Reliable and clump-forming spreader with delicate foliage. Blooms throughout the summer. 60cm × 45cm.

Dicentra spectabilis ◑ (8) Beautiful, spring-border plant with heart-shaped rose-pink flowers. Most reliable in moist but well-drained soil and part-shade. 60cm × 45cm.

Dierama pulcherrimum ○ (9) Reliable and easy only on light but moist, lime-free soil. Pink bells in late summer on arching stems above clumps of rushy leaves. 90cm × 30cm.

Euphorbia griffithii **'Fireglow'** ○ (10) is a fine cultivar with brick-red flower heads in early summer and strong, bushy, spreading growth. 75cm × 45cm. Other easy border candidates include *E. polychroma* (p. 28) and *E. wulfenii* (p. 26).

Geranium traversii **'Russell Prichard'** ○ (11) Easy, valuable, front-of-border plant; spreading silver-grey mats and magenta-pink flowers throughout summer. 25cm × 45cm +. Other indispensable hardy geraniums are mentioned on p. 34 and p. 70. Further varieties for sun or part-shade are **G. 'Johnson's Blue'** with blue flowers in late June (45cm), **G.**

ibericum platypetalum, purplish-blue flowers slightly earlier (60cm × 30cm), and **G. armenum** (shown on p. 101) which has magenta flowers with a black eye (75cm × 60cm).

Hemerocallis An essential border plant producing a prolonged succession of summer flowers and handsome rushy leaves. Adaptable and easy. Innumerable yellow, mahogany-red and pink cultivars ranging 60–100cm × 60cm. Shown here is the best pink, **'Pink Damask'** (12). See also *Hemerocallis* 'Golden Chimes' and other cultivars on p. 28.

Iris sibirica ○ Arguably the easiest and best iris species for the border. Cultivars of white, blue, plum or violet obtainable. Moist soil preferred. The illustration shows **'Purple Mere'** (13). All flower in high summer. 90cm × 30cm.

Lilium ○ Two of the easiest are the floriferous lime-loving **L. henryi** (14), which needs deep planting, and **L. regale** (15) (plant deeply also). Both can reach 2m. The stems of the former will arch over, but staking is only necessary in a windy position. Summer-flowering.

Lychnis chalcedonica ○ (16) A 90cm scarlet-flowered plant which needs light soil to thrive. Flowers in high summer. Plant 60cm apart.

Mertensia virginica ◐ (17) A beautiful, spring-flowering, spreading plant for a cool soil and part-shade. Greyish leaves die down early. 45cm × 22cm.

Peonies ○ Essential border plants. Although their burst of flowers in early summer is short-lived, their foliage persists attractively. Of the different groups and many cultivars, we show **Paeonia lactiflora 'Bowl of Beauty'** (18), 90cm × 75cm. Never disturb peonies.

Physostegia virginiana **'Vivid'** ○ (19) Deep pink flowers in early autumn. There is also a white-flowered form. 45cm × 50cm.

Platycodon grandiflorum **'Mariesii'** ○ (20) Deep blue or white swollen flower buds open to stars in summer. Well-drained

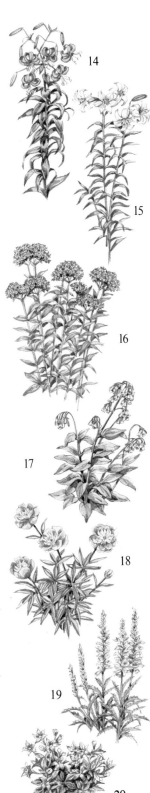

soil. 30cm × 30cm.

Polygonum Two of the most suitable are the little **P. affine 'Darjeeling Red'** (21), its little red spires of flowers produced in autumn over spreading mats. 25cm × 30cm. The other is also illustrated: **P. amplexicaule atrosanguineum** (22), its red flowers appearing over a long period from late summer onwards. Bushy growth. 120cm × 60cm.

Potentilla ○ The herbaceous potentilla is trouble-free and strong-growing. Cultivars obtainable have orange, rose-pink or yellow flowers. **'Gibson's Scarlet'** (23) is shown here. All have a long summer season in flower. 30–45cm × 30cm.

Rudbeckia **'Goldsturm'** ○ (24) Vigorous cultivar, dwarfer than most. Flowers from summer till autumn. 75cm × 40cm.

Salvia × superba **(S. virgata nemerosa)** ○ (25) A robust, long-flowering plant with violet-purple spikes in summer. 90cm × 45cm. **'East Friesland'** is a shorter cultivar at 45cm. **'May Night'**, also 45cm, begins to flower slightly earlier.

Sedum spectabile **'Autumn Joy'** ○ (26) reliable, robust plant with succulent leaves and flat heads of russet flowers in autumn. 45cm × 45cm.

Sidalcea ○ (27) Spikes of mallow-like flowers of pink or red over a long season in summer. Leave undisturbed as long as possible. 75–100cm × 45cm depending on cultivar.

Sisyrinchium striatum E:○ (28) Iris-like leaves and pale yellow spires of flowers in early summer. Good contrast to a horizontal-leafed neighbour. 50cm × 22cm.

Consider also: *Anaphalis triplinervis* (p. 30), *Anemone hupehensis* (p. 37), *Artemisia* 'Lambrook Silver' (p. 30), bergenias (p. 26), *Brunnera macrophylla* (p. 59), epimediums (p. 34), erigerons (p. 70), *Galtonia candicans* (p. 33), *Helleborus corsicus* (p. 26) and *H. orientalis* (p. 62), hostas (p. 27 and 28), kniphofias (p. 26), *Nepeta mussinii* (p. 30) and tradescantias (p. 37).

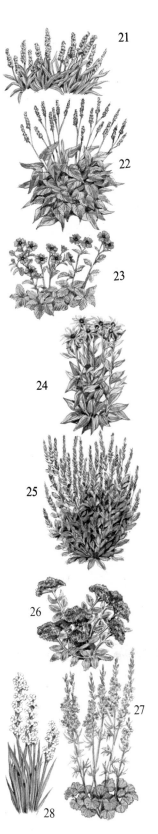

Border Perennials

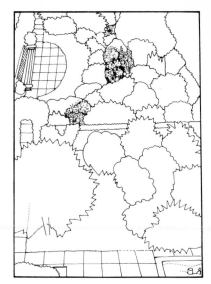

The plants on this page demand a little more attention than those on the previous list.

Alstroemeria **'Ligtu hybrids'** ○ (1) Gorgeous summer flower – carmine to cream to salmon. Spreading where happy but hard to establish. Plant container-grown subjects and never disturb. Give rich soil and twiggy support. 90cm × 30cm.

Campanula lactiflora (2) White, pink and lavender cultivars obtainable, and a rich blue called **'Prichard's Variety'**. Flowering summer, often until autumn. Moist, rich soil. Stake. Never disturb. 60–180cm × 60cm +.

Chrysanthemum rubellum ○ (3) including the buttery **'Mary Stoker'** and pink **'Clara Curtis'**, for late summer to autumn. Divide regularly and give twiggy support. 80cm × 45cm.

Delphinium Pacific Giant series (4) in pink, white or pale to darkest blue is the best, but may dwindle after a few years. 120–150cm × 60cm–1m. **'Belladonna'** varieties are shorter. Rich, moist soil and staking. Main display in summer.

Eremurus ○ Finest is *E. robustus* (5) with startling, pastel-coloured spires of flowers in early summer. The crowns and shoots are frost-tender and need protection. Don't disturb. 3m × 40cm. The yellow *E. bungei* is shorter at 1·5m.

Gypsophila paniculata ○ (6) Useful for hiding gaps left by early bloomers. The double, white **'Bristol Fairy'** and double, pink **'Flamingo'** (90cm × 60cm) may need support. Not always hardy. Best in light soil. Protect against slugs. Never disturb.

Helenium (7) Most useful cultivars are those that flower from late summer through the autumn, such as the crimson-bronze **'Bruno'** (100cm × 40cm) or the bronze-red **'Moorheim Beauty'**. Stake these taller varieties.

Kirengeshoma palmata ◑ (8) Pale yellow, autumn-flowering, Japanese plant. Part-shade and moist, leafy soil essential where it can spread. Good companion to shade-loving shrubs. 80cm × 60cm.

Lobelia cardinalis (9) Velvety red, autumn-flowering plant with bronzed leaves. Support required, and rich, moist soil. Give winter protection or lift and store. 90cm × 45cm.

Meconopsis betonicifolia LH: ◑(10) Sky-blue poppy flowers with golden anthers and hairy, glaucous leaves. Only perennial if plants are stopped from flowering in their first year: 1m × 40cm. *M.* × *sheldonii* is a richer, deeper blue, at its best in the forms **'Branklyn'** or **'Slieve Donard'**. All need cool, leafy soil and part shade. June flowering.

Monarda (11) Showy plant with flowers of red, pink, violet or white in summer to autumn. Regular division beneficial. Moist but well-drained soil. 90cm × 45cm.

Papaver orientalis (12) Showy flowers of pink, red, orange or white in early summer. Often with a black base. Stake and cut foliage after flowering. Don't disturb. 90cm × 75cm.

Phlox paniculata (syn. *P. decussata*) ◑ (13) Late summer flowers of lavender, purple, pink, red, salmon, or white. Needs moist soil and prefers part-shade. Division every three years necessary. Often menaced by eelworm. 70–90cm × 60cm.

Thalictrum dipterocarpum ◑ Lavender flowers in late summer on elegant, wiry stems. Here is the exquisite, mauve, double-flowered cultivar **'Hewitt's Double'** (14). Rich, light soil. Stake unless in very sheltered position. 180cm × 60cm.

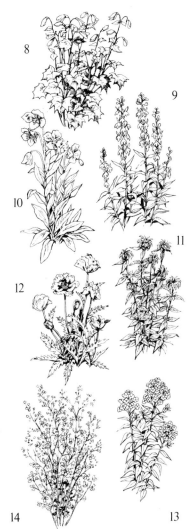

Ornamental Herbs

Give herbs an area to themselves because many self-sow furiously. But if space is limited, some are ornamental enough to merit a place in the border. All self-sowers will need sharp watching; seed-heads should be removed and seedlings which develop outside the allotted territory should be dug up. Plant herbs in sun unless otherwise stated.

Angelica (*Archangelica officinalis*) (1) Decorative in leaf and creamy flower. Perennial if stopped from flowering. Stems can be crystallised. Self-sowing. 1·5m × 60cm.

Bay (*Laurus nobilis*) E (2) A dark, aromatic-leafed evergreen shrub which lends itself to topiary. Needs shelter in a harsh winter. Height according to pruning.

Borage (*Borago officinalis*) (3) An annual with pretty, stamened, blue flowers above coarse, hairy leaves. Invasively self-sowing. 40cm × 22cm.

Chervil (*Anthriscus cerefolium*) (4) A self-sowing annual with dainty, feathery leaves which will persist through the winter if autumn sown. Useful for egg dishes. 40cm × 22cm.

Chives (*Allium schoenoprasum*) (5) Useful edging plant with pink-purple flowers. The giant variety, **A.s. sibiricum**, is more decorative. Cut leaves from base to ensure a succession of shoots. 25cm × 22cm.

Fennel (*Foeniculum vulgare*) (6) Feathery, green foliage but the bronze variety is more beautiful. Cut off golden flower-heads (unless seeds are for kitchen use) to prevent self-sowing and attain bushier plants. 1·3m × 1m.

Hyssop (*Hyssopus officinalis*) E (7) Can be used in stews and salads but now grown chiefly as a useful evergreen sub-shrub with rich blue (or pink) flowers 45cm × 45cm.

Lovage (*Levistichum officinalis*) (8) A shapely plant with purple stems and glossy leaves which give a celery tang to stews. 1·2m × 1m.

Marigold (*Calendula officinalis*) (9) An annual with a tradition as a border plant. Its orange-yellow petals can be used in salads. Invasively self-sowing. 40cm × 30cm.

Marjoram (10) The variety *Origanum vulgare* 'Aureum' has golden leaves and dusty pink flowers. 30cm × 40cm.

Parsley (*Carum petroselinum*) (11) An excellent edging plant or can be used in front-of-border groups in sun or shade. Biennial but sow annually for succession. 15cm × 15cm.

Winter savory (*Satureia montana*) E (12) An evergreen sub-shrub with small mauve flowers, its leaves used for stews, salads and fish. 30cm × 30cm.

You can supplement this list with violas, pansies and nasturtiums whose flowers are edible. All these are possible front-of-border candidates. And don't forget rosemary (p. 39), sage (p. 39), golden balm (p. 28) and thyme, of which the lemon, the caraway and the common thyme (*T. vulgaris*) are the best cooking varieties.

Never plant mint in the border, however. Its running rootstock is highly invasive and is best confined to a tub or self-contained corner.

Colour Borders

One approach to designing distinctive borders and beds is to limit their flowers to those of a single colour or to a restricted colour range. It is an idea which was explored and elaborated to brilliant effect by the garden designer Gertrude Jekyll (1843–1935) and many of her theories on this subject have remained influential though their provenance has often been forgotten and their disciplined application relaxed.

Her most ambitious schemes involved colour which was carefully graded across the entire spectrum in a border, but nowadays such spectacular set-pieces as these are largely confined to a few major gardens which are open to the public. Displays of this nature demand spacious settings and involve labour-intensive plants, so are ill-suited on both counts to most contemporary gardens (even supposing the owner has the knowledge and chromatic confidence to tackle them).

Instead it is more usual today for an owner to devise a border of just one or several colours. The choice may be purely a matter of personal preference, though other factors might well exist which recommend one choice above another.

In the case of borders which are planted to display a single colour, white is arguably the first candidate for either a shaded woodland arrangement against a dark backcloth or for a border which is seen often or mainly at dusk, for pale flowers will gleam in twilight. (It was for this reason that white flowers were grown in the great Hindu gardens which were visited by their owners in the cool evenings.) In contrast, blue borders are tranquil and cooling in a hot position, though they are the first to lose their identity when daylight fades. Red borders are dramatic and luxurious, always a dominant feature whatever the surroundings. Massed yellow will make a garden seem sunshiny even on a dull day, an effect which (as Miss Jekyll once pointed out) can be reinforced in large gardens if they can be approached from an area of trees and shrubs. Nor must green be omitted as a colour in its own right, for a green border with all its subtle variations of tone is the most refreshing and restful of all.

These single colour borders appear at their best when the dominant hue is interpreted somewhat elastically. Thus a white border will shimmer if its icy colours are softened by touches of cream, pale yellow, blush, blue-grey and set off by deepest green. Yellow is enlivened by orange and lime. A red border is lightened by the addition of a little apricot and enriched by deep purple blooms and dark foliage plants.

In such cases, the appropriateness of these colour associations is based on the application of a few simple principles. Firstly, hues which are next to each other in the spectrum (for example, red-violet, red and red-orange) will complement and reinforce each other. Secondly, one of the most harmonious of all associations is achieved by combining white, a pure colour and its tint – such as deep and pale blues and white, or pink, crimson and white. Furthermore, triads (groups of three colours) are appealing to the eye, especially in the case of blue and yellow flowers against green foliage – the most harmonious grouping, for green is made up of blue and yellow.

Indeed, the colour of foliage must always be taken into account, for these colour rules are being applied to garden-making, far removed from pure arts. Grey-leafed plants, for example, can be used in their own right to build a tonal picture with flowers of white, lilac, purple or pink. Dark-leafed shrubs and perennials will make a foil to paler colours.

In fact, it is the foliage which remains the one constant even when you devise a border which changes its hue with the seasons. To give the simplest example, a yellow, white and green spring border becomes a crimson, pink, white and green summer border, as different groups of flowers succeed one another, though the foliage remains mainly the same.

Opposite are examples of two colour borders which have been shown as alternatives within the same hedged, south-facing area in a garden. The red border has the more conventional arrangement of the two, but the dominant colour has been intensified by violet flowers and dark-foliage plants. The white border, which has been divided into beds with gravel intersections, includes touches of pale yellow, and blue- and grey-leafed plants and many of its flowers have been chosen for their scent. These borders have been composed of plants shown and described elsewhere in the book.

The planting plan of the white border is shown on page 79, and the red border is given on page 80.

Edge-Breakers

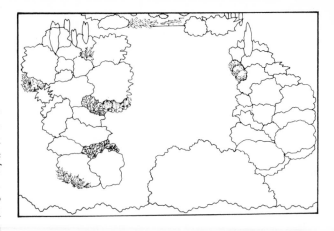

No bed or border ever looks luxuriant or even comfortable if it stops short of its edge. The plants seem self-conscious, as though they are only perching there but have not taken root and settled in. This stiff appearance can be avoided if you plant along the edge the kind of spreading subjects which will spill over the boundary. The most useful plants are evergreen, but there are also many herbaceous candidates with lush, bold leaves and arching stems which will be effective from May through to October. For the shrub border, the most valuable are either the less rampant prostrate evergreen shrubs or else those under 1m with a rounded habit which will sit like hummocks at and over the edge. To simplify mowing the adjacent lawn lay a line of paving (mowing-stones) at the edge of the bed below the level of the grass.

PERENNIALS FOR SUN

Campanula alliariifolia (1) Clump-forming perennial with long, heart-shaped, grey-green leaves and stems of ivory flowers for many weeks in summer and intermittently in autumn. 45cm ×45cm.

Erigeron ○ (2) Several useful dwarf cultivars, all with long-flowering pink, blue, violet or white daisy flowers in summer over a mat of leaves. Here is the deep pink 'Forster's Liebling', 45cm × 40cm.

Geranium macrorrhizum 'Album' (3) Ground-cover plant with scented leaves colouring in autumn. White flowers in early spring. Content in sun or shade. The type plant is pink-flowered. 30cm × 40cm.

Hakonechloa macra 'Albo-aurea' ○ (4) A golden Japanese grass with some green and fawn variegation. Yellowish inflorescence in late summer. A dazzling low edger. 25cm × 30cm.

Liriope muscari E:○ (5) Valuable, labour-saving plant with rushy evergreen leaves and spikes of small violet flowers over a long period late in the year. 30cm × 22cm.

Consider also: *Acanthus mollis* (p. 34), *Anthemis cupaniana* (p.101), *Carex morrowii* (p.58), geraniums (p. 34, 64, 70 and 101), *Helictotrichon sempervirens* (p.58), hemerocallis (p. 28 & 64), *Nepeta mussinii* (p.30),

Stachys lanata (p.30), *Stipa gigantea* (p. 58), veratrum (p. 58).

PERENNIALS FOR SHADE

Asarum europaeum E:● (6) Spreading ground-cover with glossy, richly evergreen leaves (and insignificant flowers in spring). 10cm × 30cm.

Ferns E:◑ The evergreen *Polystichum aculeatum acutilobum* (7) is illustrated here with its lacy, finely divided fronds, one of the best of the ground spraying ferns. Needs well-drained soil. 50cm × 60cm. The deciduous *Athyrium* (p. 26), Hart's Tongue Fern (E) (p. 38) or *Polystichum setiferum plumoso divisilobum* (E) (p. 58) are also all first choices.

Heuchera (8) Virtually evergreen leaves surmounted by dainty flowers of white, cream, pink or shades of red in early summer. 40–90cm × 30cm.

Saxifraga fortunei ◑ (9) Shiny, bold leaves with a dark red reverse and sprays of white flowers in autumn. 30cm × 30cm. **S. umbrosa** is also illustrated (10), the evergreen 'London Pride', which is accommodating wherever it is grown. Pale or deep sprays of pink, starry flowers in spring. **S.f. 'Rubra'** is larger than the type and there is also a variegated form. 25cm × 22cm.

Tiarella cordifolia E:◑ (11) Foaming white flowers in spring over ground-covering foliage. **T.**

wherryi is also suitable, differing from the former in having a non-running rootstock and creamier flowers. 25cm × 30cm.

Consider also: *Alchemilla mollis* (p. 26), bergenia (p. 26), *Campanula* 'Stella' (p. 37), *Helleborus foetidus* and *H. orientalis* (p. 62), hostas in variety (p. 26 and 28), *Tellima grandiflora* (p. 34).

SHRUBS FOR SUN
Hebe albicans E: ○ (12) There are a number of valuable small, evergreen hebes for this position. This one makes a spreading, grey, small-leafed mound with white flower-spikes in summer. 60cm × 1·3m. **Hebe 'Carl Teschner'** is also good, forming much lower mounds of shiny green leaves with violet flowers in later summer: 30cm × 45cm. See also *H. rakaiensis* (syn. *subalpina*) on p. 35.

Iberis sempervirens 'Snowflake' E: ○ (13) Popular and accommodating shrublet with mounds

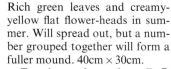

of evergreen leaves and dead white flowers massing the plant in spring. It is larger than *I. commutatum* shown on p. 22. 22cm × 60cm +.

Phormium cookianum (syn. *P. colensoi*) E: ○ Strictly a grassy-leaved perennial but usually catalogued with shrubs. It is shorter and has more flexible foliage than the tall *P. tenax*, shown on p. 27. Numerous cultivars exist with leaves varying from green to variegated red, green and white. Yellowish flowers on spikes in late summer. **'Cream Delight'** (14) is illustrated with a green margin to its cream leaves. 75cm × 70cm.

Picea pungens glauca 'Procumbens' E (15) Stunningly blue, prostrate spruce which is suited to the front of a conifer- or rock-border. Its stiffness makes it an alien in the conventional setting of the mixed, deciduous border. 15cm × 1m.

Santolina virens 'Alba' E: ○ (16) As useful but less common than the grey santolina on p. 31.

Rich green leaves and creamy-yellow flat flower-heads in summer. Will spread out, but a number grouped together will form a fuller mound. 40cm × 30cm.

Teucrium chamaedrys E: ○ (17) An old evergreen favourite with pink flowers during a long period in summer over dark leaves. 30cm × 30cm.

Consider also: *Artemisia arborescens* (p. 58) and *A. stelleriana* (p. 30), helianthemum (p. 25 and 39), *Helichrysum splendidum* (p. 31), lavender (p. 31), *Ruta graveolens* (p. 30).

SHRUBS FOR SHADE
Azalea E:LH:◑ The most suitable azaleas for edging positions are the spring-flowering, evergreen varieties which form spreading bushes of 60cm–1·2m. There are seven main groups and a colour range of white, pink, red, orange, lavender and violet. **'Hinomayo'** shown here (18), is a Japanese hybrid, belonging to the Kurume group, an old and reliable variety massed with clear pink flowers in late spring. 60cm × 1m.

Danae racemosa E:● (19) Arching stems with rush-like sprays of evergreen leaves (strictly leaf-stems, not leaves). Recommended for its graceful habit. 1m × 60cm.

Hedera helix 'Conglomerata' E (20) Although this is an ivy, it does not climb but leans stiffly on the ground. Dark green leaves, reducing in size the higher that they clothe the erect shoots. 60cm × 40cm.

Rhododendron E:LH:◑ Of the thousands of this genus under cultivation, the most useful in a front-of-border position are those which have a neat, mounded habit. Of these, **R. williamsianum** (21) is an exquisite species with heart-shaped leaves and pale pink bell flowers in spring. 60cm × 1·3m. **R. russatum** (22) is a less spreading plant with deep violet flowers in spring and a compact, rounded habit of growth. 70cm × 70cm.

Consider also the smaller, bushy hydrangeas such as 'Preziosa' (p. 36), *Skimmia japonica* (p. 61) and *Viburnum davidii* (p. 35).

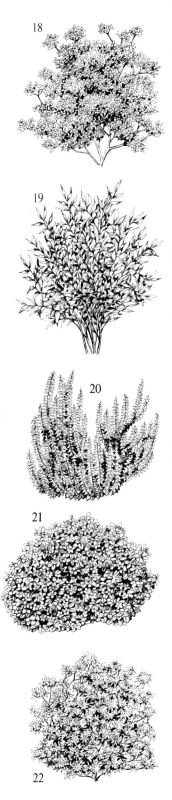

Pool Borders

For general notes on the composition, planting and design of the pool border see pages 51–53, but below is a selection of the finest aquatic and marginal plants. In addition to these, you will need submerged, oxygenating plants which are introduced in the pool to keep the water fresh. All the following are suitable; *Anacharis* (syn. *Elodea*) *canadensis* (rampant), *Callitriche verna*, *Ceratophyllum*, *Lagarosiphon major* and *Myriophyllum*.

Water-lilies are in a class of their own, for most require deeper water than any of the aquatics listed below. Except for the miniature varieties like *Nymphaea pygmaea* (for a water-depth of 7·5cm), the garden pool varieties must have a minimum depth of 30–45cm and the more vigorous will need 1·2m–1·5m. Choice depends therefore on the depth of water and width of the pool (the vigorous varieties have too large a leaf spread for a small pool), before colour can be considered. However, fine reds include 'Escarboucle' (with flowers up to 20cm across) and the carmine 'James Brydon', both for a water depth of about 60cm. 'Gladstoniana' is a magnificent white with golden stamens, for deeper water of 75cm–1m. 'Pink Opal' is coral-pink and for shallower pools of 30–45cm depth. As a rule of thumb, a water-lily bearing the prefix of *Marliacea* will be a cultivar of outstanding quality. An open, sunny position is essential or the flowers will not open.

Gunnera manicata (1) Giant-leafed waterside subject for large areas. Its inflorescences appear in May. Establish in spring and cover crowns in winter with its (1·5m) dead leaves as frost-protection. 3m × 3m. *G. scabra* is smaller at 1·8m.

Iris Among the best for marginal planting are *Iris kaempferi* (2) (summer flowers in blue, mauve, pink, red or white), gorgeous but difficult, needing plenty of water whilst growing but dryer conditions in winter; also acid soil. 90cm × 30cm. Handsome alternatives include the yellow native for larger pools, *I. pseudocorus* (1·1m × 30cm) and the creamy *I. ochroleuca* (1·2m × 40cm). *I. sibirica* (see page 64) is equally easy. The violet-blue or white *I. laevigata* (11) is a true aquatic and is best grown in shallow water. 45cm × 30cm.

Lysichitum americanum (3) is for boggy soil or very shallow water. Arum-type yellow flowers in spring (or white in the smaller variety, *L. camtschatcense*) are followed by imposing clumps of leaves. 1·2m × 1m.

Osmunda regalis LH (4) Splendid deciduous, autumn-colouring fern for moist, acid soil with erect fronds up to 2m but usually less. Prefers shade but will usually stand full sun in soil full of humus. Usually 1·2m × 45cm.

Peltiphyllum peltatum (5) Handsome, spreading foliage plant for moist soil round larger pools. Pink sprays of flowers in spring followed by large round leaves, usually colouring well in autumn. Good companion for grassy-leaved plants. 100cm × 60cm.

Pontederia cordata (6) Spear-shaped leaves and spikes of blue flowers in July/August on a true aquatic to be planted in water up to 15cm deep. 50cm × 40cm.

Primula An important group for moist soil. Varieties like *P. beesiana* (carmine), *P. bulleyana* (gold), *P. japonica* (white, crimson and pink) and *P. pulverulenta* (white and rose shades), all flower in early summer; 50cm × 30cm. For summer, there is the golden *P. helodoxa* (1m × 40cm). For late summer, the 75cm × 40cm yellow *P. florindae* (7) and the yellow *P. sikkimensis* (40cm × 30cm). The most suitable varieties for spring are the white, mauve or ruby drum-head *P. denticulata* (25cm × 30cm) and the lime-intolerant deep pink *P. rosea* (10cm × 20cm).

Scirpus tabernaemontani 'Zebrinus' ○ (8). A highly ornamental banded sedge for planting in a container of pond mud, placed in shallow water; or simply in moist soil as a marginal. Grows by creeping rhizomes. 1·8m × 60cm.

Trollius Beautiful marginal plants with yellow or orange globular flowers in early summer. There are many good cultivars including **'Goldquelle'** (9) shown here, though the species are also worth planting. 60–90cm × 30–50cm.

***Zantedeschia aethiopica* 'Crowborough'** ○ (10) Fairly hardy arum lily flowering for a long season, summer to autumn. A plant for the moist border, but it will also grow in shallow water. In either case, its tubers should be protected from frost. 90cm × 60cm.

The following plants, described elsewhere in the book, are also suitable for planting in moist soil beside the pool; *Aruncus sylvester* (p. 64), astilbe (p. 64), *Astrantia carniolica* (p. 64), bamboos (p. 59 and 98), *Camassia quamash* and *C. leichtlinii* (p. 32), *Fritillaria meleagris* (p. 32), hemerocallis (p. 28 and 64) hosta (p. 26 and 28), *Kirengeshoma palmata* (p. 66), *Leucojum aestivum* (p. 32), *Lobelia cardinalis* (p. 66), mimulus (p. 75), rodgersia (p. 34).

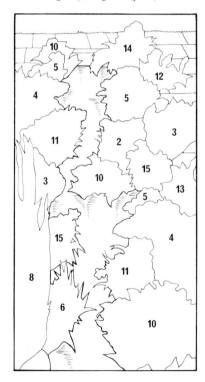

Example of a lushly-planted canal pool.

The numbers in the plan refer to the plants opposite except: 12. *Hosta* 'Honeybells' 13. *Hosta sieboldiana* 'Elegans' (p. 26) 14. *Hemerocallis* 'George Cunningham' 15. *Hemerocallis* 'Pink Damask' (p. 65).

Hardy Annuals, Half-Hardy Annuals and Biennials

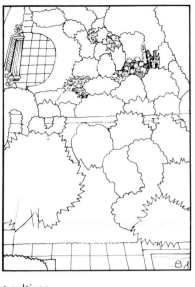

For the negligible cost of a few packets of annual seed, you can transform a garden. But cheapness isn't the only virtue of these annuals. They will also give you a more rapid display than any other border plant; the majority have a brilliance that is unrivalled; and, equally important, many are virtually foolproof to grow. Moreover their variety makes them highly adaptable, some suited to fill a summer border in a new garden, others to occupy gaps after a death or before permanent plants have grown to their allotted span. Some will act as edging plants, a few are suited to the rock garden, others will flourish by the pool margin.

Biennials are arguably more work, but they include not only valuable subjects for spring beds, but some of the best loved of all border plants.

* indicates it can be sown in autumn as well as spring.

HARDY ANNUALS

Atriplex hortensis rubra ○ (1) Highly ornamental red-leafed and stemmed foliage plant suited to red borders. Grows up to 2m(× 30cm) flowering and fruiting. Stake.

*Echium (*E. vulgare*) ○ (2) Blue (also rose, mauve or white), long-flowering, easy, bushy plants for edges or the rock garden. 30cm × 30cm.

*Eschscholzia ○ (3) Showy single or double flowers of red, pink, orange or yellow with a long season. Good for poor, dry soils. 15–37cm × 15cm.

*Larkspur ○ (4) The Imperial is the variety usually grown, tall and branching plants with white, pink or violet-blue flowers; 120cm. The Hyacinth variety blooms a fortnight earlier, but usually produces only a single spike and is shorter at 75–90cm. There are also dwarf varieties at 45cm. Plant 30–45cm apart.

Lavatera ○ (5) Bushy, floriferous plants of 60–120cm with large white, rose pink or cerise blooms. Plant 60cm apart.

Linum grandiflorum rubrum ○ (6) Most graceful, easy-to-grow plant bearing silky, crimson flowers with a dark eye. There is also a white variety. Mass in groups. 35cm × 20cm.

*Nigella ○ (7) Beautiful, easy annual with feathery foliage and white, rose, dark blue or pale blue flowers (this is the finest cultivar, called **'Miss Jekyll'**), followed by handsome seed pods. 37cm × 15cm.

*Phacelia campanularia ○ (8) Intense blue flowers on a low, quickly-flowering plant for edgings or rock gardens. 22cm × 15cm.

Other hardy annuals included in the book are *Dimorphotheca aurantica*, godetia, Love-lies-bleeding, nasturtium and sweet peas; see pages 40–41.

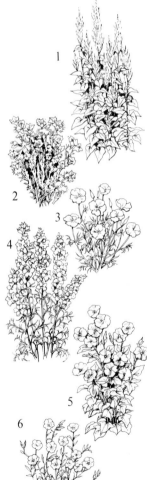

HALF-HARDY ANNUALS

Anagallis linifolia ○ (9) Bushy, dwarf plant flowering through summer and autumn with gentian-blue flowers with a red eye. Good edger or rock plant. 15cm × 15cm.

Cleome spinosa ○ (10) Tall, bushy and spiny plant. The type has mauve flowers, but the white (**'Helen Campbell'**) and the pink (**'Pink Queen'**) are superior. Both flower for several months. 100cm × 60cm.

Cosmos ○ (11) Graceful fernyleafed plants with large single flowers of crimson, rose or white over a long season. Also gold or orange variety with two rows of petals growing to 70cm × 40cm.

Dahlia ○ A large range of hybrids with single or double flowers in a full colour range and from 37–120cm × 45–90cm can be raised as HHAs. We show here

the pompon type (12). At the end of the season, lift the tubers and store in frost-free surroundings.

Kochia trichophylla (13) Pale green bush, reddening in autumn. Grow in groups as foliage clumps or as an edging hedge. 60cm × 45cm.

Mimulus ○◑ (14) Beautiful branching plants for a moist border or a pool margin. Dwarf varieties suit the rock garden. Usually pink, red or ruby-marked yellow. 10–30cm × 15–30cm.

Nemesia ○ (15) Compact plants – quick to flower though the display is short. For edging or the rock garden. Massed blue, white, primrose, yellow, orange, pink or red flowers. 22–30cm × 15–22cm.

Nicotiana (16) Indispensable, perfumed flowers of white, lime-green, crimson or dusky pink though some forms will not open their blossoms fully in daylight. Good in part-shade. The tall varieties have more grace. 45–90cm × 30–60cm.

Salpiglossis ○ (17) The most beautiful of all annuals with veined, velvet flowers of rich red, gold, rose, blue or mahogany. 45–90cm × 30–40cm.

Salvia patens ○ (18) One of the finest tender salvias with intense gentian-blue flowers. Lift the tubers and store like dahlias. 60cm × 37cm.

***Tithonia* 'Torch'** ○ (19) Substantial plant with burnt-orange flowers from summer through autumn. It needs a hot position. Stake. 120cm × 45cm.

Verbena ○ (20) Edging plants with a long flowering season, weather-resistant. Purple, lavender, red, pink or white flowers; 15–30cm. *V. venosa* has rosy-purple flowers and produces tubers which can be lifted and stored. 45cm × 30cm.

Other suitable half-hardy annuals include antirrhinum, arctotis, gazania, lobelia, petunia, and *Ricinus communis*; see pages 40–41.

BIENNIALS
Canterbury bell (*Campanula medium*) ○ (21) Old-fashioned plant with white, blue or pink, bell or cup-and-saucer flowers in June. 75cm × 37cm.

Hollyhock (*Althaea rosea*) ○ (22) Better as a biennial than perennial, as it is subject to rust disease. Single or double white, rose, yellow, apricot or crimson flowers. Stake in open. Up to 2·2m × 45cm.

Iceland poppies (*Papaver nudicaule*) ○ (23) Silky, pastel flowers of white, yellow, orange, pink or rose, flowering from May on. Most graceful plant in all respects. 45cm × 15cm.

Stocks (*Matthiola*) ○ (24) There are annual stocks, but the biennial is the Brompton Stock, branching plants in shades of white, pink, carmine, mauve or purple with a rich scent. Flowering time is May and June. 45cm × 37cm.

Sweet William (*Dianthus barbatus*) ○ (25) Scented flowers for June/July of white, pink, scarlet or crimson. 45–60cm × 30cm. There is also a dwarf variety which can be grown as an annual.

Verbascum ○ Two dominant and handsome mulleins for the border are *V. bombyciferum* (26) (syn. *V. broussa*) with white, hairy leaves and lemon flower spikes to 1·8m; and *V. olympicum* with darker yellow flowers to 2·5m, also silver foliage. Both make rosettes of leaves the first winter from which the flowering spikes arise. Plant 60cm–1m apart.

Wallflowers (*Cheiranthus cheiri*) ○ (27) Scented, spring-bedding plants in flame, primrose, brown, blood-red, pink, purple or ruby. 15–45cm × 15–30cm.

See also foxgloves on p. 38 and *Onopordon arabicum* on p. 27.

Rock and Dry-Wall Gardens

Anyone who wants to grow an enormous variety of plants yet has only a limited space at his disposal, might consider building either a rock or a dry-wall garden. The choice depends partly on appearances, partly on the amount and type of stone to hand and, not least, on the time you have for maintenance.

A rock garden tends to be more difficult to site successfully and more time-consuming to look after. Informality is its essence, its origin being an imitation of the natural formations of stone to be found in the wild. It follows that it looks happiest when concealed from formal or over-civilised surroundings – an impracticable ideal for most garden-owners. Similarly, the most suitable stones to use are large, natural, local and undressed (uncut).

Whichever kind of stone is used, its lay-out should appear natural which is easier if it is made on sloping ground. Avoid all neat and dinky arrangements which resemble nothing so much as "rows of false teeth in the dentists' shops" as the 19th century writer, William Robinson, put it. For the sake of the plants avoid, too, overhanging stones which prevent light or rain reaching flowers beneath them; if possible tilt them backwards.

Good weed-free soil, mixed with leaf-mould or compost (and lightened with horticultural grit or silver sand, if necessary for free drainage) should be used; but if you are planting lime-haters and your soil is insufficiently acid, give them a large pocket of ericaceous compost.

Finally, be prepared to weed this kind of garden. You cannot rely on many weed-suppressing, ground-cover plants in this position, as they will swamp choicer varieties.

Dry-wall gardens, whether two-flanked to form a raised bed or single-flanked to retain an earth bank, are much more labour-saving. They require little or no weeding and many of the plants can be tended without stooping. They also provide a marvellous way of growing many plants in little space near a house or in formal surroundings.

The stones used (whether natural, artificial or re-constituted) should be even and flat, but since they are much smaller than those in the rock garden, they are easier for the do-it-yourself enthusiast to handle. They must be built up to form a batter (a backward slope) and the plants, positioned in large pockets of the same kind of soil as above, placed at the bottom of a vertical crevice so that rain will reach them.

The example illustrations on the opposite page show a sunny rock garden in summer, above, and the shady side of a dry-wall garden in spring, below. Most of the plants are evergreen so that the 'gardens' will be clothed in winter. And, equally important, a balance has been struck between those plants which trail, those which tuft up and those which form mats.

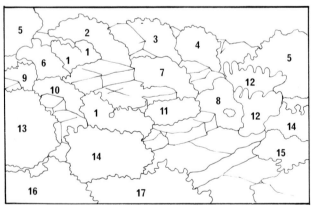

Planting plan of the rock garden.

1. *Dianthus deltoides* (p. 25)
2. *Phlox subulata* 'Oakington Blue Eyes' (p. 25)
3. *Arabis blepharophylla* (p. 24)
4. *Dryas octopetala* (p. 22)
5. *Cotoneaster congesta* (p. 35)
6. *Allium beesianum* (p. 32)
7. Cheddar Pink (*Dianthus gratianopolitanus*) (p. 39)
8. *Raoulia australis* (p. 25)
9. *Sempervivum* 'Commander Hay' (p. 39)
10. *Sempervivum arachnoideum* 'Laggeri' (p. 24)
11. *Thymus serpyllum* 'Coccineum' (p. 24)
12. *Othonopsis cheirifolia* (p. 25)
13. *Campanula portenschlagiana* (syn. *muralis*) (p. 37)
14. *Armeria maritima* 'Vindictive' (p. 24)
15. *Antennaria dioica* 'Rosea' (p. 25)
16. *Tanacetum densum* 'Amanum' (p. 25)
17. *Acaena* 'Blue Haze' (p. 25)

Planting plan of the dry-wall garden.

1. *Hedera helix* 'Glacier' (p. 96)
2. *Primula* 'Wanda' (p. 62)
3. *Saxifraga umbrosa* (p. 70)
4. *Festuca glauca* (p. 34)
5. *Pulmonaria rubra* (p. 62)
6. *Pulmonaria angustifolia azurea* (p.62)
7. *Arenaria balearica* (p. 24)
8. *Othonopsis cheirifolia* (p. 25)
9. *Cytisus × kewensis* (p. 35)
10. *Hedera helix* 'Conglomerata' (p. 71)
11. *Hepatica × ballardii* (p. 62)
12. *Iberis* 'Snowflake' (p. 71)
13. Primrose (*Primula vulgaris*) (p. 38)
14. *Dryopteris borreri* (see *D.b.* 'Cristata' p. 26)
15. *Blechnum tabulare* (p. 58)
16. Hart's Tongue Fern (*Phyllitis scolopendrium*) (p. 38)
17. *Erythronium dens-canis* 'Rose Queen' (p. 32)
18. *Omphalodes verna* (p. 38)

Planting Plan of Garden 4: Cottage Garden (Page 48)

1. Morello Cherry tree (p. 54)
2. *Trachelospermum asiaticum* (p. 57)
3. *Sophora tetraptera* (p. 56)
4. *Clematis armandii* (p. 20)
5. *Daphne odora* 'Aureomarginata' (p. 63)
6. Bay (*Laurus nobilis*) (p. 67)
7. *Chaenomeles × superba* 'Crimson and Gold' (*Chaenomeles* on p. 57)
8. *Cotoneaster horizontalis* (p. 57)
9. *Hydrangea macrophylla* 'Mme. Mouillère' (see Hydrangea on p. 36 and p. 61)
10. Golden Marjoram (*Origanum vulgare* 'Aureum') (p. 67)
11. *Aster × frikartii* (p. 64)
12. *Narcissus poeticus* 'Actaea' (see Daffodils and Narcissi on p. 32)
13. Hyssop (p. 67)
14. *Cistus × purpureus* (p. 60)
15. *Phormium cookianum* 'Cream Delight' (p. 71)
16. Lavender 'Hidcote' (p. 31)
17. Lemon thyme (p. 67)
18. *Iberis commutatum* (p. 22)
19. *Salvia × superba* 'May Night' (p. 65)
20. *Cistus × pulverulentus* (p. 39)
21. *Artemisia abrotanum* (p. 93)
22. Caraway thyme (p. 67)
23. *Viola odorata* (p. 62)
24. *Rosmarinus officinalis* (p. 39)
25. *Hebe rakaiensis* (syn. *H. subalpina*) (p. 35)
26. *Alchemilla mollis* (p. 26)
27. *Helleborus orientalis* (p. 62)
28. *Primula auricula* (p. 37)
29. *Helleborus foetidus* (p. 62)
30. *Hamamelis mollis* 'Pallida' (p. 63)
31. *Bergenia* 'Ballawley' (p. 26)
32. *Hemerocallis* 'Pink Prelude' (p. 65 for Hemerocallis)
33. *Carex morrowii* 'Variegata Aurea' (p. 58)
34. *Sedum spectabile* 'Autumn Joy' (p. 65)
35. *Paeonia lactiflora* 'Bowl of Beauty' (p. 65)
36. *Hemerocallis* 'Pink Damask' (p. 65)
37. *Iris foetidissima* 'Variegata' (p. 22)
38. Iris Pacific Coast hybrids (p. 39)
39. *Helleborus corsicus* (p. 26)
40. Tulip 'Angel' (see Tulip in general on p. 32)
41. Tulip 'Greenland' (as above)
42. *Buxus sempervirens* 'Suffruticosa' (p. 93)
43. Chives (p. 67)
44. Spinach
45. *Thymus vulgaris* (p. 67)
46. Fan-trained peach tree (p. 54)
47. *Itea ilicifolia* (p. 57)
48. Purple sprouting broccoli
49. Chervil (p. 67)
50. Parsley (p. 67)
51. Winter savory (*Satureia montana*) (p. 67)

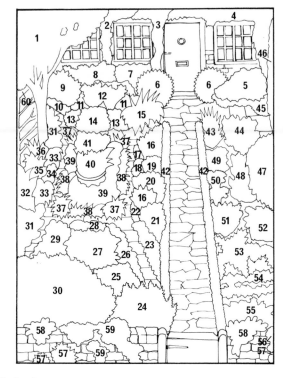

52. Rhubarb
53. Globe artichoke (*Cynara scolymus*) (p. 27)
54. Broad beans
55. Angelica (p. 67)
56. *Saponaria ocymoides* (p. 25)
57. Sempervivum (particular varieties on p. 24 and p. 39)
58. *Othonopsis cheirifolia* (p. 25)
59. *Arabis alpina* (p. 24)
60. Espalier apple tree (p. 54)

Planting Plan of Garden 5 (Page 49)

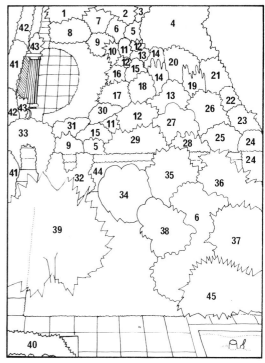

1. *Fatsia japonica* (p. 27)
2. *Aralia elata* 'Variegata' (p. 59)
3. *Pyracantha* 'Shawnee' (p. 28)
4. *Genista aetnensis* (p. 55) underplanted with *Hebe armstrongii*, not visible (p. 93)
5. *Campanula lactiflora* 'Prichard's Variety' (p. 66)
6. *Phlomis fruticosa* (p. 93)
7. *Buddleia* 'Lochinch' (p. 31)
8. *Hebe cupressoides* (p. 93)
9. *Perovskia atriplicifolia* (p. 31)
10. *Veratrum album* (p. 58)
11. *Nigella* 'Miss Jekyll' (p. 74)
12. *Lilium regale* (p. 65)
13. *Cleome spinosa* 'Helen Campbell' (p. 74)
14. Delphinium Pacific Giant 'Blue Jay' (p. 66)
15. *Gypsophila paniculata* 'Bristol Fairy' (p. 66)
16. *Helictotrichon sempervirens* (p. 58)
17. *Artemisia arborescens* (p. 58)
18. *Alstroemeria* 'Ligtu Hybrids' (p. 66)
19. *Verbascum olympicum* (p. 75)
20. *Eucalyptus gunnii* (p. 58)
21. Climbing Rose 'Iceberg' (see p. 20 for Climbing Roses)
22. *Clematis orientalis* (p. 56)
23. *Clematis macropetala* (p. 21)
24. *Hedera helix* 'Goldheart' (p. 28)
25. *Abutilon vitifolium* (p. 57)
26. *Rosa rubrifolia* (syn. *R. glauca*) (p. 59)
27. *Ferula communis gigantea* (p. 58)
28. *Berberis thunbergii* 'Rose Glow' (p. 59)
29. *Weigela florida* 'Variegata' (p. 59)
30. *Echium* 'Blue Bedder' (p. 74)
31. *Anthemis cupaniana* (p. 101)
32. Golden Hop (*Humulus lupulus* 'Aureus') (p. 28)
33. *Lonicera japonica* 'Halliana' (p. 20)
34. *Cortaderia* 'Gold Band' (p. 58)
35. *Cornus alba* 'Elegantissima' (p. 59)
36. *Mahonia lomariifolia* (p. 27)
37. *Cytisus albus* (p. 57)
38. *Stipa gigantea* (p. 58)
39. Rowan tree (*Sorbus acuparia*) (Other *Sorbus* on p. 55)
40. *Hedera helix* 'Cavendishii' (See ivies on pp. 20, 28, 96)
41. *Hedera colchica* 'Dentata' (p. 20)
42. *Hedera colchica* 'Dentata Variegata' (p. 20)
43. *Nicotiana* 'Evening Fragrance' (p. 75)
44. Lawson Cypress 'Green Hedger' (p. 91)
45. *Arundinaria viridistriata* (p. 59)

The White Border (Page 69)

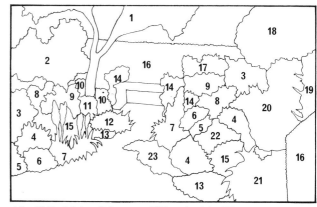

1. *Eucalyptus niphophila* (p. 55)
2. Rose 'Penelope' (p. 95)
3. *Phlomis fruticosa* (p. 93)
4. White lavender (p. 31)
5. *Tradescantia* 'Osprey' (p. 37)
6. *Ruta graveolens* 'Jackman's Blue' (p. 30)
7. *Yucca filamentosa* (p. 27)
8. *Cleome spinosa* 'Helen Campbell' (p. 74)
9. *Lilium regale* (p. 65)
10. *Helleborus corsicus* (p. 26)
11. *Artemisia absinthium* 'Lambrook Silver' (p. 30)
12. Pink (*Dianthus* 'Mrs. Sinkins') (See other forms of *Dianthus* on p. 25 and p. 37)
13. *Artemisia stelleriana* (p. 30)
14. *Nicotiana affinis* (p. 75)
15. *Hebe albicans* (p. 71)
16. Yew (*Taxus baccata*) (p. 23)
17. *Philadelphus* 'Manteau d'Hermine' (p. 57)
18. *Pyrus salicifolia* 'Pendula' (p. 31)
19. *Onopordon arabicum* (p. 27)
20. *Magnolia stellata* (p. 60)
21. *Agapanthus campanulatus* 'Albus' (p. 64)
22. *Cistus × loretii* (p. 60)
23. *Tanacetum densum* 'Amanum' (p. 25)

79

Planting Plan of Garden 6   (Page 50)

1. *Acer palmatum* 'Senkaki' (p. 55)
2. *Juniperus chinensis* 'Aurea' (p. 54)
3. *Agapanthus* 'Headbourne Hybrids' (p. 64)
4. *Prunus* 'Amanogawa' (p. 55)
5. Floribunda rose 'Escapade' (p. 36)
6. *Acer palmatum* 'Dissectum' (p. 59)
7. *Acanthus mollis* (p. 34)
8. *Rhus typhina* 'Laciniata' (p. 55) underplanted with *Liriope muscari* (p. 70), not visible.
9. *Sorbus hupehensis* (p. 55)
10. *Geranium macrorrhizum* 'Album' (p. 70)
11. *Hemerocallis* 'Golden Chimes' (p. 28)
12. *Rhododendron yakushimanum* (p. 60)
13. *Miscanthus sinensis* 'Zebrinus' (p. 58)
14. *Hydrangea macrophylla* 'White Wave' (See other forms of *H. macrophylla* on p. 61)
15. *Sorbus scalaris* (p. 55)
16. *Saxifraga fortunei* (p. 70)
17. *Danae racemosa* (p. 71)
18. *Sambucus racemosa* 'Plumosa Aurea' (p. 29)
19. *Fatsia japonica* (p. 27)
20. *Magnolia salicifolia* (p. 55)
21. *Hydrangea villosa* (p. 61)
22. *Rhododendron russatum* (p. 71)
23. *Rhododendron* 'Praecox' (p. 60)
24. *Viburnum betulifolium* (p. 61)
25. *Polystichum aculeatum acutilobum* (p. 70)
26. *Arundinaria murieliae* (p. 98)
27. *Pinus wallichiana* (p. 88)
28. *Prunus subhirtella* 'Pendula' (p. 19)

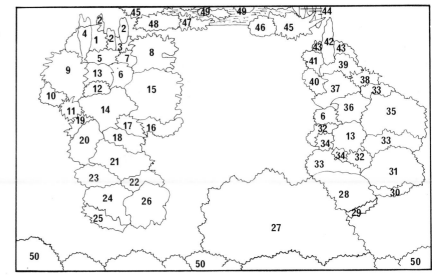

29. *Brunnera macrophylla* (see the alternative variegated form on p. 59)
30. Golden Marjoram (*Origanum vulgare* 'Aureum') (p. 67)
31. *Cotoneaster frigida* (p. 55)
32. *Rosa rugosa* 'Frau Dagmar Hastrup' (p. 61)
33. *Hydrangea arborescens* 'Grandiflora' (p. 94)
34. *Hosta sieboldiana* (p. 26)
35. *Koelreuteria paniculata* (p. 18)
36. *Tamarix pentandra* (p. 95)
37. *Magnolia × soulangiana* 'Alba' (p. 18)
38. *Paeonia lutea ludlowii* (p. 57)
39. Hybrid musk rose 'Cornelia' (p. 60)
40. *Hebe albicans* (p. 71)
41. *Helianthemum* 'Wisley Pink' (See other cultivars of *Helianthemum* on p. 25 and p. 39)
42. *Cupressus sempervirens* (p. 54)
43. *Salvia × superba* 'May Night' (p. 65)
44. *Juniperus communis* 'Hibernica' (p. 54)
45. *Juniperus × media* 'Pfitzerana' (p. 23)
46. *Pinus mugo* 'Pumilio' (p. 23)
47. *Picea pungens glauca* 'Procumbens' (p. 71)
48. *Juniperus sabina tamariscifolia* (p. 35)
49. *Geranium traversii* 'Russell Prichard' (p. 64)
50. Tops of woodland trees at rear of garden.

The Red Border (Page 69)

1. *Cotinus coggygria* 'Royal Purple' (p. 59)
2. *Phormium tenax* 'Purpureum' (p. 27)
3. *Magnolia liliflora* 'Nigra' (p. 60)
4. *Rosa rubrifolia* (syn. *R. glauca*) (p. 59)
5. Yew (*Taxus baccata*) (p. 23)
6. *Lobelia cardinalis* (p. 66)
7. *Fuchsia magellanica* 'Riccartonii' (p. 61)
8. Rose 'Lilli Marlene' (p. 61)
9. *Salvia × superba* 'East Friesland' (p. 65)
10. Bronze fennel (*Foeniculum vulgare*; p. 67)
11. *Dahlia* 'Bishop of Llandaff' (p. 74)
12. *Atriplex hortensis rubra* (p. 74)
13. *Hemerocallis* 'Stafford' (p. 64)

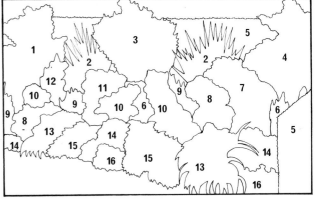

14. *Berberis thunbergii atropurpurea* 'Nana' (p. 93)
15. *Acer palmatum* 'Dissectum Atropurpureum' (p. 59)
16. *Potentilla* 'Gibson's Scarlet' (p. 65)

Plants for Hedges, Backgrounds and Features

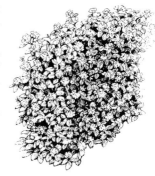

Plants for Hedges, Backgrounds and Features

Dominant plant features of this type should not usually be afterthoughts. They are the first fundamentals to which you add the smaller furnishings like beds and borders. If you are re-designing your whole garden or working on a blank canvas, here is your starting-point. If you simply want to add a hedge or a main feature to an existing garden, then be prepared for the possibility that it may dictate further changes.

The fact is that, even though such features may form backgrounds to other plants in the garden, they are part of its actual structure and therefore a key element in its design.

This is especially true of hedges. These are just as important as the partitions of a house, defining not only a room's extent, but its shape as well. They have a number of additional purposes to fulfil too. They give privacy, they screen unwanted views, they protect against intruders, and they give wind shelter also. They are actually far more effective against wind than solid walls, for they filter its force instead of blocking it and thereby causing undue turbulence and eddying.

The type of hedge you choose is an important decision. The possibilities are enormous (there are over 80 suggestions in the following pages), yet your requirements may narrow this array to a handful. You must decide whether you want it to be evergreen or deciduous; to flower, fruit or berry; to back a border, front a garden, or define a path. Do you want extreme formality or the irregularity of free growth? Would you like the type of hedge which is suited to incorporating 'windows' and 'doorways'? Do you want a circular or curving hedge? How often are you prepared to clip it and how much room do you have? On a more practical note, how much are you prepared to pay, for different varieties can vary greatly in price. These are only a few of the factors to be considered. Other points are raised in the following pages, and examples of hedges chosen for particular purposes are shown in the two gardens overleaf.

These two gardens demonstrate as well the use of other large, permanent and decorative features. They include trees which are planted as specimens, dominating a particular area of a garden. They show screening blocks, climbers planted as individual features, arbours or pergolas and, not least, topiary of the simplest type to the most complex and magnificent in maturity. Some of these features are functional as well as beautiful, but all of them can give a garden a memorable and individual stamp.

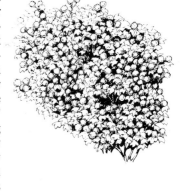

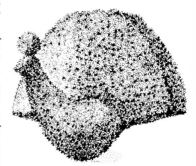

Garden 7

Windy, Hillside Site

Any garden high on a hillside is likely to be exposed to wind and needs sheltering plants. Its position may also reduce its privacy, but the cottage garden here is typical of many in that it enjoys views which should not be blocked. The owners must tackle the following problems.

1. Some form of screening is needed against cottages above, below and to the side of the garden.
2. A chain fence separates but does not hide the garden from the lane.
3. There is nowhere satisfactory to sit out. The paved area beside the house is exposed and insufficiently self-contained.
4. The 'orchard' of apple and pear trees is old and unproductive, notably three ancient trees near the cottage down the hill.
5. The owners want to retain the informality of the grassed areas, yet would still like some barrier between these and the house.

Solutions

1. Clumps of screening trees are planted to give the cottage privacy from other houses. All the trees are wind-resistant and short enough not to block off more distant rural views. Two of the clumps (beside and behind the house) are evergreen and semi-evergreen as these plantings are essential to privacy. See SCREENS, pages 98–99.
2. The chain fence beside the lane is replaced by a tough evergreen hedge which is dense and thorny enough to deter dogs and intruders. See EVERGREEN HEDGES, pages 90–91.
3. The paved area to the side of the house is given its own separate identity and greater shelter by the boundary of a slim, evergreen hedge. An arbour is erected in the far corner in a position to catch maximum sun and enjoy the best views. See PERGOLA AND ARBOUR PLANTS, pages 104–105.
4. The unproductive fruit trees are festooned with climbers to make them at least decorative. See CLIMBERS AND THEIR HOSTS, pages 96–97.
5. A deciduous hedge is planted which is not too formal yet separates the roughly grassed 'orchard' area from the more civilised parts. See DECIDUOUS HEDGES on pages 94–95.

The garden is shown in high summer. Planting plan on page 106.

Garden 8

Large, Dull and Flat

Herbaceous borders, expanses of grass, a rose hedge emphasise the drawbacks of this plot, not its assets.
1. Although the garden is large and therefore full of potential, it remains boring, partly because it can all be seen at a glance and lacks mystery.
2. Unrelieved flatness is another reason for its dullness.
3. The herbaceous borders are dormant in winter. A rose hedge provides winter views only of twigs.
4. The amount of mowing is a heavy chore.

Solutions

1. The first step is to divide a garden this size into different areas, several entirely enclosed. This disguises its overall squarish shape.
2. The yew hedges used for this purpose also redeem the lack of height. TREES FOR SPECIMENS (pages 88–89) play a major part in changing the levels.
3. Out go the herbaceous borders and rose hedges. Instead, TOPIARY (pages 102–103) provides all-the-year interest. Privet hedge is replaced by yew, which is also used for the topiary-tableau in one of the enclosures. In addition, the stilt hornbeam hedge rising

above the 1·6m front wall gives privacy. Plants at the foot of hedges (see PLANTS FOR THE FOOT OF HEDGES, pages 100–101) soften the formality.
4. Lawn is confined to just two enclosures and the rest of the ground is gravelled or paved. Low hedges (see HEDGES FOR BORDERS AND LOW DIVIDERS, pages 92–93) define the separate areas.

Although the whole garden is highly formal, once the training of the topiary and stilt hedges is completed, upkeep is restricted to the annual trimming of topiary yews, hedges and hornbeams in late summer.
The picture shows the garden in late winter/very early spring. Planting plan on page 106.

Hedges and Features: Preparation, Planting and Aftercare

Planning is essential. The easiest way of choosing the site for a hedge is to test out its line in advance with string stretched along pegs. (Most hedges follow a straight line, but if you want a curved or circular hedge, use a centrally placed batten and attach to it a string lead which can be swivelled in an arc.) Then, visualise how the fully-grown hedge will look in this position; or, alternatively, take a photograph of the area and draw in the hedge on the print. When planning the site, take into account any eyesores that should be screened. Consider, too, where you need your openings and, if there is to be more than one aperture, are they lined up if necessary? Finally, make sure that you allow room for the hedge's thickness; as much as 1m from the nearest plants in a border, and not less than 60cm distance from a path.

Calculating the number of plants

This estimate will depend on the intervals required between the plants. Remember that the first and last plants don't go in at the very end of a row, but at a distance of half the usual interval, to allow for their eventual spread. The number of plants will also vary (obviously) if you plant a double row (or even treble) of staggered plants with the purpose of making an extra-strong barrier.

Digging the soil

When you have decided on the site, kill off all perennial weeds in the area with a weed-killer that does not poison the soil. Then, dig a trench along the line of string and pegs to a spade's depth and about 1m width for a single row of plants. (Increase this width to 1·5m if you will be planting a double row.) If the soil is seriously waterlogged, the soil must be dug to double the spade's depth and, without bringing the lower spit of subsoil to the upper spit, insert plastic drainage pipes and rubble. Otherwise, the hedge will simply perish. To give any hedge a good start, work old dung, compost or bonemeal into the trench.

Planting

You can plant deciduous hedges any time between October and March so long as the soil isn't frozen or sticky with rain. Plant evergreens in early autumn or mid–late spring when the soil is warmer. In a cold or exposed spot, evergreens will also need some protection against icy, scourging winds, to prevent them suffering from wind-burn which can be fatal. In this case, erect in advance polythene sheeting (supported on stakes) on the wind-exposed side of the planting line.

To ensure you plant your hedge in an absolutely straight (or perfectly curved) line, make an indentation in the earth or nick out the soil to a spade's depth immediately below the taut string you have stretched on pegs. Keeping accurately to this indentation, plant each shrub to the depth of its original soil line, having spread out the roots on bare-rooted plants. Put the finest soil around the roots before filling in the rest of the hole with earth. Firm down the soil around each plant to prevent it suffering from wind-rock. Tall, thin plants may need to be tied to a stake and, in this case, the pole should be fixed stoutly in the planting hole in advance.

Watering and mulching

The young hedge will have to be kept watered in dry weather, and this is especially important for evergreens which can die in a spring drought. Mulch the hedge also to conserve moisture (see page 53 for details).

Clipping

The most suitable pruning time/s for each variety of hedge are given in the description for each individual shrub. But as a general principle, those that need hard clipping in their early years to induce lush growth at the base, can be cut back in March of the following year if they are spring planted, or 18 months after autumn planting. Otherwise, let the leader or growing shoot continue until the desired height is reached, but trim the side shoots regularly.

Always make sure that the base of the hedge is broader and bushier than the top. This produces a sloping effect which is called a batter. It allows light and air to reach the lower branches which encourages strong growth; it prevents gappiness at the base; it results in greater stability.

Hedges lend themselves also to a variety of decorative treatments. You can give them 'doors' and 'windows'; you can top them with topiary; you can trim them to form stilt hedges which look like slim, green boxes on poles. Guidance on these specific forms of training is given on pages 102–103.

Feeding

All trimmed hedges respond to being fed, for severe clipping makes demands on the shrubs. To keep them in peak condition, give them old manure or compost, bonemeal or liquid manure in the spring.

Reviving an old or neglected hedge

Some evergreen hedges will simply have to be scrapped, because they are unable to refurbish themselves from old wood when cut back. *Lonicera nitida* is one common example of this disadvantage. But the toughest evergreens, of which yew is a notable illustration, can be cut back (even into old wood) and will clothe themselves in new shoots and green leaves so long as one side is trimmed first and the second side only tackled when the first has revived.

If the hedge has a gap, plant a youngster in the space, but only in renewed, well-dug and manured soil. If the gap is a very narrow one, you can take the simpler course of tying together growths from the plants either side of the hole. Again, feed them well to encourage new and bushy growth.

Specimen trees

There is often a case for planting an isolated tree or grouped trees of a single species, not because they will slip comfortably into their surroundings, but in order to form a dominant feature in themselves. A selection of possibilities is shown on pages 88–89, ranging from a 2m pygmy to giants of their race which can only be accommodated in very large gardens.

Siting the tree to best effect will depend perhaps on the fall of sunlight, views from or to the house, as well as its surroundings. But in any self-contained area forming a rectangle or a rough square, the tree will look more comfortable if it is planted off-centre, at a point on the diagonal between the centre and one of its far corners. Here it will appear composed yet at ease within its framework, rather than a man-made blockage in the middle.

Climbers and their hosts

It is a waste to use some of the choicer specimen trees as supports for climbers which may eventually obscure them, but some of the less distinguished or plain shabby can be transformed by growing through their branches the more rampant clematis, rambling roses and other twiners. Possibilities and planting method are suggested on pages 96–97 and three examples shown in Garden 7.

Trees are not the only subjects for such treatment and a list of suitable shrubs (whether free-standing or grown against walls) is provided on page 97.

Whatever the position, the host (support) plant must be either mature or else sufficiently developed to have established a stout framework, otherwise it may perish, throttled to death by a climber growing at a faster pace than itself. The climber should be planted at some distance from the main trunk or stem of the tree or shrub to protect its roots from the uphill task of establishing themselves in soil that is already exhausted by the sitting tenant.

Vigorous climbers may have to be controlled and pruned, otherwise they are likely to envelop (and perhaps finally kill) an insufficiently large host plant.

Topiary

Topiary is one of the most ornamental and individual additions to any garden, though it is slow to make its presence felt, since training must be taken in stages over a number of years.

The most elaborate type of design is shown in Garden 8, where formal shapes, birds and animals are housed like a menagerie in their own enclosure. Patterns of this kind, executed in yew, may easily take twenty years before they are fully developed. However, simple, clipped balls (such as those of golden privet in Garden 2 and the bay spheres flanking the door in Garden 4) are completed in a few years and are certainly more suited to most gardens than the more complex and eccentric designs.

Details of preparation, training and aftercare are given on pages 102–103, along with information about simpler forms of clipped plants, such as the stilt hedge, doorways and windows.

Pergolas, pleached alleys and arbours

These features can also be a form of topiary, for the earliest arbours were made of clipped hawthorn; and clipped yew tunnels and arbours can still be seen in ancient gardens. Even now, pleached alleys (walks formed of interlaced trees, their trunks and branches trained over iron supports) are still planted; sometimes with pears or apples, more usually with the rapid-growing laburnum. Usually, however, the framework for these features (a solid structure of metals, masonry or timber) is designed to be festooned by rapid-growing climbers. For further details see pages 104–105.

Pergolas are not always easy to accommodate in a garden, for they need to be connected on at least one of their sides to some kind of wall, if they are not to appear random additions. One solution is to erect them against the façade of the house overlooking the garden (as in Garden 1), where they will act as shady cloisters. In this position, however, the placing of the horizontals must not block easy access to any repair work required by the windows above. Or else they can cover a path at the side of the garden, so long as it leads purposefully from one point to another.

Arbours are simpler to position and there is reason to have more than one in all but the smallest garden, each planted to climax into flower or fruit at a different season, each positioned to face a different aspect so that morning and afternoon sun can be equally enjoyed.

Trees for Specimens

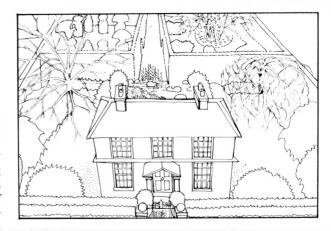

In general, plants look most comfortable when grouped, for few varieties are large or distinctive enough to hold the stage by themselves. There are certain trees, however, which would be robbed of their beauty and/or individuality if crowded. These kinds (such as weeping trees) must be grown as isolated specimens. Other kinds are equally good on their own or in small groups only of their own variety. Some of these trees are ultimately giants and are out of court for any garden less than an acre. Others are small even at maturity yet have quite as much presence.

All deserve careful siting which throws into relief their particular features, whether colour, shape, habit or winter outline. Each needs room around it so that, as it develops, it can remain a star.

CONIFERS

***Cedrus atlantica* 'Glauca'** E (1) Only for large gardens. The wide popularity of this blue-grey cedar has meant that it is too often ill-sited in cramped surroundings. Bears barrel-shaped cones to 7·5cm long. Quick growth. 30m.

Gingko biloba (2) Marvellous tree which is one of the main choices for a large garden. A deciduous conifer which is the only survivor of an important family of trees in existence 160 million years ago. Held sacred in the East and found planted by Buddhist temples. Exquisite ribbed foliage, yellowing in autumn. Slow growth. 25m.

Picea brewerana E (3) Another very beautiful conifer called 'Brewer's Weeping Spruce', which is hung with deep green curtains of 2m long branchlets. Slow growing. 15m. (***Picea smithiana*** has similarly drooping branchlets, but these are not quite so long. Bears purplish cones up to 17·5cm long. A much taller and quicker tree to 30m.)

Pinus montezumae E (4) Equally dramatic pine, but ill-suited to cold areas. It has stiff, blue-grey needles which are 18–25cm long and cones which can equal this length. Reddish-brown bark. 20m.

Pinus wallichiana (syns. ***excelsa, griffithii***) E (5) Fine, fast-growing and more adaptable pine, though not for shallow chalk, with blue-grey-green needles, 20cm long, and curving cones which can be yet longer. Soft, almost feathery appearance. 30m.

Pseudolarix amabile LH (6) The deciduous Golden Larch is slow-growing, but develops into a most graceful pale-green conifer whose leaves turn soft gold then rust, before falling in November. Impressive on lawns or against a dark background. 12m.

Taxodium distichum LH (7) The Swamp Cypress is another deciduous conifer whose leaves bronze and then turn rust in autumn before falling. Late into leaf in spring. Only for large gardens where it is suited to wet soil. If grown near water, it will develop 'knees', woody projections arising from the roots. Slowish to 30m.

Tsuga canadensis 'Pendula' E (8) Bizarre and even monstrous in growth, this is the low, mounded, weeping form of the Eastern Hemlock. Tolerant of limy soil. Best as the dominant feature in intimate surroundings. Very slow to 2m.

BROAD-LEAFED TREES

Acer platanoides 'Drummondii' (9) Variegated maple, best displayed against a dark background. Quick growth. Remove any shoots which tend to revert to plain green. 12m.

Betula jacquemontii (10) In the finest forms, it has the whitest bark of all the birches. Again, wonderful against a dark background. Thrives, like the following, in light soil. 14m.

Betula pendula 'Youngii' (11) Densely-leaved, domed, weeping tree reaching, at most, 8m. Its silvery bark is scarcely visible through its foliage.

Cercidiphyllum japonicum (12) A tree of rapid growth, noted for its autumn colour which is usually scarlet when young, and gold or pink when older. Plant where it can be admired in winter for the symmetrical outline of its bare branches. Moist, good soil. 15m.

Corylus avellana 'Contorta' (13) The slow-growing Corkscrew Hazel whose leaves yellow in autumn. Again, plant where it can be viewed in winter for its tortured branches, bearing catkins in early spring. Ultimately 5m.

Davidia involucrata (14) Of no great significance in leaf or habit until at around ten years old, it starts to produce the great white bracts in May which earn it the name of the Handkerchief Tree. Any soil. 15m.

Fagus sylvatica 'Purpurea Pendula' (15) Dramatically weeping, mushroom-headed form of the Purple Beech. Very slow-growing but makes a fine glistening copper mound even when young. 7m.

Fraxinus excelsior 'Pendula' (16) Large, wide-spreading, vigorous weeping tree which makes a magnificent lawn specimen. Late to break into leaf in spring. 15m.

Liriodendron tulipifera (17) Subject only for a large garden. Saddle-shaped foliage turning a rich yellow in autumn and greenish flowers (with a soft orange band) looking like an opened tulip produced in June on trees which are at least 15 years old. Quick growth. (There is also a variegated form.) 30m.

Robinia pseudoacacia 'Inermis' (18) The Mop-Head Acacia has a distinctively neat, round head. Ideal subject for formal surroundings where even the tree should add to the precision. Unlike the type plant, non-flowering. 8m.

Salix caprea 'Kilmarnock' (syn. 'Pendula') (19) A very small, weeping tree with a stiff, vertical branch habit. It is shown here in winter, but its leaves are up to 10cm long, greyish beneath. 3m.

Salix matsudana 'Tortuosa' (20) Fastest growing of all trees here, the Contorted Willow makes a cone with twisted branches and curled twigs. Narrow leaves with a greyish underside. 20m.

See also; *Catalpa bignonioides* 'Aurea' (p. 29). *Cornus controversa* 'Variegata' (p. 55), *Cupressus sempervirens* (p. 54) a possible subject for grouping in its own kind, *Eucalyptus niphophila* (p. 55), *Gleditsia triacanthos* 'Sunburst' (p. 29), *Koelreuteria paniculata* (p. 18), *Pinus pinea* (p. 19), *Prunus subhirtella* 'Pendula' (p. 19), *Robinia pseudoacacia* 'Frisia' (p. 29).

Evergreen Hedges

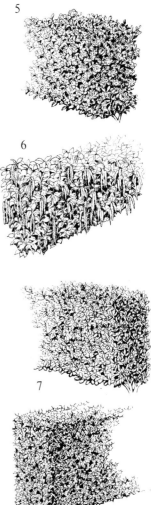

Tall, dense, evergreen hedges are virtually living walls and should be used as such. At all times of the year, they form barriers within a garden and redoubtable boundaries around it.

Some of those listed below are far too big for small gardens, as they will outgrow their station on reaching maturity. Others, however, can be kept clipped into slimness and should be preferred where space is short. Some flower and fruit, others give a more self-effacing display but lend themselves to intricate trimming to provide doorways, windows and topiary shapes. Quick-growing varieties are more demanding, as they require clipping three or even four times a year. The slow hedges make you wait, but repay this disadvantage by needing only one annual clip. Varieties with very large leaves must be hand-trimmed with secateurs to avoid mutilating their foliage, and in such cases, the length of hedge should be taken into account. A few varieties are toxic to stock and should not be grown where animals can reach the leaves.

Aucuba japonica E (1) Handsome hedge especially in the variegated form or berrying (female) clones. Tolerant of poor soil and shade. Large leaves need careful trimming with secateurs. Plant 1m apart. 2.5m.

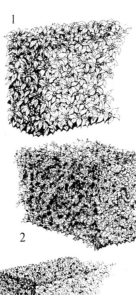

Berberis × stenophylla E (2) Vigorous, dark, dense hedge with thorns to keep out intruders. Gold flowers in April. Plant 45cm apart. Clip after flowering. 2·5m.

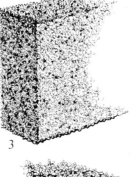

***Buxus sempervirens* 'Handsworthensis'** E (3) Makes a high, dark green formal hedge up to 4·5m if necessary and is suited to topiary. Noted for its aromatic leaves. Needs well-drained soil and is good on chalk. Unsuited for backing borders as its roots tend to be invasive. Plant 45cm apart. Trim in early June and again, if needed, in September. The form ***B.s.* 'Elegantissima'** has cream-margined leaves and reaches 1·2m.

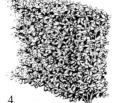

Cotoneaster franchetii E (4) A beautiful hedge which can be kept slim, bearing white flowers in spring and coral berries. Sage-green leaves with a silver underside. Plant 45cm apart. Trim after growth has finished. 2·5m.

Escallonia E (5) Good seaside hedges for withstanding wind and salt-spray, but the hardier varieties are also suitable inland. ***E.* 'Langleyensis'** is the toughest with rosy-pink flowers in summer and a spreading habit to 2m. ***E.* 'Ingramii'** is taller with pink flowers. ***E. macrantha*** has cherry-red flowers, but is fit only for mild districts. Plant 1m apart and prune after flowering.

Garrya elliptica E (6) Californian shrub making marvellous hedge in sheltered positions. Glaucous leaves and 15cm silvery catkins in February. The female's catkins are much shorter, so ensure you buy the male plant, the best clone of which is called **'James Roof'**. Plant 1m apart. Prune in spring. 2·5m.

Griselinia littoralis E (7) Establish in spring on a well-drained site for it is not ideally suited to cold areas. Good on chalk. Glossy apple-green leaves, handsome in the plain or cream-variegated forms. Plant 1m apart. Prune in spring. 2·5m.

Holly E Many hollies make excellent hedges in sun or shade and on any soil, but the thornier varieties are unsuited to a situation where hand-weeding is necessary. *Ilex × altaclarensis* **'Camelliifolia'** is dark green and almost spineless; *Ilex* **'Golden King'** (see p. 29) is also nearly spine-free. At the other extreme is *Ilex aquifolium* **'Ferox Argentea'** (8), the silver Hedgehog Holly, with spines on the upperside as well as around its leaves. Margins and spines are creamy-white. Plant about 45–60cm apart. Ultimate height around 8m if required.

Lawson Cypress (*Chamaecyparis lawsoniana*) E Coniferous hedge which is good in wind and part-shade. Many cultivars of different shades from blue to bright green to gold. Normal rate of growth is about 60cm a year, but **'Fletcheri'** (with grey-green foliage, bronzing in winter) (9) is a much slower cultivar, reducing the need to clip. Plant about 1m apart.

Leyland Cypress (*× Cupressocyparis leylandii*) E (10) Another coniferous hedge with phenomenally speedy growth needing at least three trims a year. Soon outgrows its station. Plant 1m apart.

Olearia macrodonta E (11) Reasonably hardy shrub with holly-like leaves, sage-green above and silvery beneath. Profuse display of white daisy flowers in June. Best on acid soil. Plant in spring 1m apart. Clip after flowering. 2m.

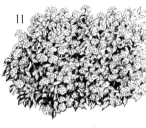

Osmanthus delavayi E (12) Rather slow-growing with small, dark leaves, but of value for its small, very fragrant white trumpet flowers in April. Plant about 45cm apart, and clip after flowering. 2m.

Phillyrea decora E (13) Related to the above, this shrub is tough and hardy with glossy, leathery leaves. Fragrant white flowers in

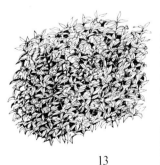

clusters in April. Plant 45cm apart and clip after flowering. 2m.

Prunus lusitanica E (14) The Portugal Laurel makes an excellent hedge with glossy, dark green leaves and slim racemes of creamy flowers in June. Good subject for simple topiary. Plant about 60cm apart. Clip after flowering. 3m.

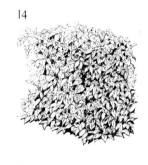

Quercus ilex E (15) The Holm Oak is a giant, but makes a fine dark green hedge, though growing corpulent from slow beginnings. Plant pot-grown subjects as much as 2m apart if wanted. Prune in late spring. Almost any ultimate height above 2·5m.

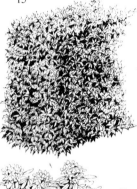

Rhododendron ponticum E:LH:◑ (16) The common rhododendron with mauve flowers in late spring. Needs acid soil and self-sows and layers where suited. Bushy and spreading. Toxic to stock. Plant 1m apart. 3m.

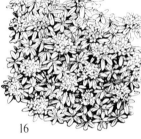

Thuja occidentalis E (17) Slowish-growing conifer thriving in any well-drained soil. Many cultivars of green or gold. Needs clipping only once a year. **T. plicata** is a faster-growing hedge needing two clips, but is suited to a narrow space as it can be kept slim. Plant 60cm apart. 3m or more.

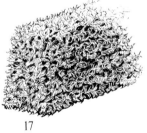

Viburnum tinus E (18) Dark, shiny leaves and pinkish-white flower clusters in winter. Plant 45cm or more apart and trim after flowering is finished in spring. 3m.

In addition to the listed varieties, the following plants should be considered for hedging; bay (p. 67), laurel (p. 22), *Lonicera nitida* (p. 22), pyracantha in variety (p. 28), *Taxus baccata* (p. 23).

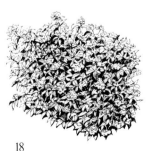

Hedges for Borders and Low Dividers

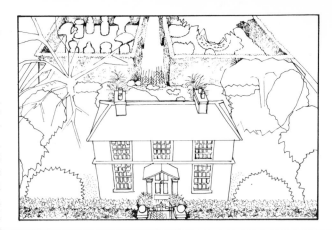

Any hedge which is used to back a border should be a variety which lends itself to formal clipping. Other factors matter too. Its roots should not be unduly invasive and greedy. Its width is important: a slim border needs a slim hedge; a larger border can share its space with a corpulent hedge like yew. Colour can be another consideration, for several of the purple-leafed varieties listed below are sometimes used to provide a contrast to pale flowers before them. One practical factor is especially important; as a general rule, confine yourself to those hedges which need only one annual clip. It is a major drawback not only to prune but pick up the fallen twigs at the back of a border more than once a year.

Most of the small-leafed or coniferous evergreens on pages 90–91 are also candidates.

HEDGES FOR BORDERS

Beech (*Fagus sylvatica*) (1) Probably the best formal, deciduous hedge and good on all well-drained soils. Its leaves turn russet in autumn and, if pruned in August, will remain throughout the winter. Good topiary subject. Plant 45–60cm apart and don't trim the leaders until the desired height is reached. Copper beech (2) makes a good background to a red border. Up to any height.

Chaenomeles × superba **'Pink Lady'** is shown on p. 57, but only makes a short hedge. Illustrated here is **'Rowallane'** (3) making a brilliant display in spring. Plant 45cm apart and clip after flowering. 1·5m.

Cotoneaster simonsii (4) Deciduous but colouring brilliantly in autumn when it also bears large vermilion berries which persist into the winter. It is vigorous and requires two clips a year, but this is offset by the fact that it can be kept very narrow in little space. Plant 30cm apart. Up to 2·5m.

Hawthorn (*Crataegus monogyna*) (5) Not for formal surroundings, but makes a good, cheap, clipped hedge in the country. Thorny, tough, tolerant of any soil and adaptable to topiary. White flowers in late spring and dark red fruit in autumn. Plant 30cm apart and trim in late autumn. 4m.

Hornbeam (*Carpinus betulus*) (6) A strong, dense hedge resembling beech, to which it is far superior on heavy, wet soils. Retains its withered donkey-brown leaves throughout the winter if clipped in late summer. Plant 45–60cm apart. Up to 5m if necessary, but don't trim the leaders until the right height is reached.

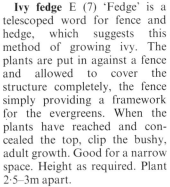

Ivy fedge E (7) 'Fedge' is a telescoped word for fence and hedge, which suggests this method of growing ivy. The plants are put in against a fence and allowed to cover the structure completely, the fence simply providing a framework for the evergreens. When the plants have reached and concealed the top, clip the bushy, adult growth. Good for a narrow space. Height as required. Plant 2·5–3m apart.

Prunus cerasifera **'Pissardii'** (or **'Nigra'**) (8) Small tree (shown on p. 55) which can be grown as a vigorous, bushy hedge. At its finest in spring when starred with pale pink flowers, but its foliage, first ruby then deepening to black-purple, is a useful contrast to a pale border near it. Unfortunately needs clipping three times a year and needs careful siting for maximum convenience. Plant 75cm apart. 3·5m.

LOW DIVIDERS

All low dividers are only for use in cultivated areas, otherwise infiltrating weeds will soon overpower them. They vary in height from a few inches to 1·3m. They cannot be used for screening, but are excellent for edges, to provide a frame, or even a pattern within whose outline different plants can be grown (on the model of the old knot gardens).

Artemisia abrotanum (9) Feathery, fragrant-leafed plant. Plant in spring 30cm apart and prune twice yearly for a formal appearance. 60cm–1m.

Berberis thunbergii atropurpurea **'Nana'** (10) Reddish-purple foliage turning scarlet in autumn on neat 'edging' hedge. Plant 30cm apart, clip once a year. 40cm.

Buxus sempervirens **'Suffruticosa'** E (11) The edging Box which can be kept clipped to a few centimetres. Plant 15–22cm apart and trim in early summer, and again if needed in autumn. 60cm.

Erica erigena (syn. *mediterranea*) E Bushy, lime-tolerant, March–May flowering heathers, varying from 60cm–2m high. Foliage is green, grey or gold, and flowers are rose, pink or white. The illustration shows **'Brightness'** (12). Plant 30cm apart and trim after flowering. See also *E. × darleyensis* (p. 63).

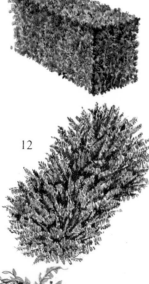

Fuchsia magellanica **'Riccartonii'** (13) is the hardiest of all varieties, making a beautiful informal hedge in sheltered gardens. Plant 37–45cm apart and trim in early spring if necessary. 1·2m.

Hebe E : ○ One of the best is *H. armstrongii* (14), a hardy, olive-gold whipcord type (which means its leaves resemble those of a cypress) with small white flowers in summer. Plant 30cm apart. Little pruning. 60cm. *H. cupressoides* is a blue-green whipcord hebe with tiny milk-blue flowers. 1m. Of the broad-leafed hebes, *H. brachysiphon* **'White Gem'** (15) is suitable, with a round habit and white flowers, 1m; and *H.* **'Autumn Glory'** (16) flowering June–October. Plant 37cm apart, trim in spring.

Phlomis fruticosa E : ○ (17) Rather lax, spreading, evergreen shrub with soft grey-green foliage and yellow-ochre whorled flowers in early summer. Prune firmly after blooming by cutting stem below flowers to keep the bush compact. Light, well-drained soil preferable. 1·2m (× 2·5m if not pruned hard). Plant 75cm apart.

Potentilla fruticosa (See also p. 36.) Shown here is **'Tangerine'** (18) which is smothered in flowers throughout the summer. Plant 40cm apart. Informal hedge but trim in winter if required. 60cm.

Ulex europaeus **'Plenus'** E (19) The double variety of the yellow gorse, making an impenetrable hedge. Good on poor, sandy soils. Plant pot-grown plants 37cm apart and prune after flowering in May. 1·2m.

Consider also: hyssop (p. 67), lavender (p. 31), sage (p. 39), santolina (p. 31), *Teucrium chamaedrys* (p. 71). Rosemary (p. 39) is also admirable but the variety 'Fastigiatus' ('Miss Jessop's Variety') is most suitable.

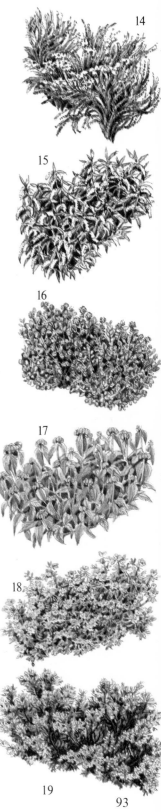

Deciduous Hedges

The other category of hedge which can make an ornamental screen or division is the deciduous hedge formed of flowering or foliage shrubs. Its effect is at the opposite extreme from the dark and severe architecture of most formal boundary or border hedges. Many of the varieties are allowed to grow fairly freely, or, if pruned, given only a slight trim rather than carved into a rectangular block. The tougher, larger varieties will make powerful windbreaks. The more floriferous and ornamental are better treated as garden features in their own right, perhaps, for example, bordering a grass walk where they serve to replace a border, being spreading, linear and colourful. Some are even sometimes used as boundary shrubs around a front garden but, being deciduous, provide inadequate cover in winter. But, wherever they are placed, nearly all these colour hedges need siting with care. The massed colours of some flowers can be overpowering and even offensive if placed near hot competition.

Blackthorn (*Prunus spinosa*) (1) A tough, suckering boundary hedge and windbreak which comes into its own along a country lane. Starry white flowers in early spring followed by black sloes. Plant 30cm apart. Prune after flowering and later in the year. 4m.

Caragana arborescens (2) Little used but one of the most attractive hedges. Small, bushy tree of Siberian origin which can be kept shrubby, enduring all soils and utmost exposure. Apple-green leaves and yellow-pea flowers in early summer. Plant 75cm apart and trim after flowering. 2·5m.

Cornus alba 'Spaethii' (3) succeeds in any soil. Golden variegated leaves and the bonus of red twigs in winter. 2·5–3m. *C. stolonifera* 'Flavirama', a rampant suckering shrub for wet soil, has plain green leaves but olive-yellow winter twigs. 2m. (See also *C. alba* 'Elegantissima' on p. 59.) Plant 60cm apart and prune late winter or early spring.

Deutzia scabra (4) Adapting to partial shade or sun and making a pretty hedge in any of its forms,

especially **'Plena'**, bearing double white flowers with a dark pink exterior. Plant 75cm–1m apart and thin after flowering in June. 2·5m.

Genista tenera ○ (5) A hedge of dazzling impact with brilliant golden sprays of flowers in high summer on a large, wide spreading bush. Plant 75cm apart. Trim after flowering but not into the old wood, only to the base of the flowering shoots. Needs full sun and plenty of room. 3·5m high and wide.

Hydrangea arborescens **'Grandiflora'** ◑ (6) bears great domes of greenish-white flowers in August through till autumn. Inclined to loll and is best against support like a low wall. Plant 60cm–1m apart and trim in early spring. 1·5m. See also *H. macrophylla* 'Ami Pasquier' and other bushy mophead or lace-cap cultivars (p. 61) which make showy hedges in mild areas; and, in colder districts, *H. paniculata* 'Grandiflora' also on p. 61.

Hypericum patulum **'Hidcote'** Semi-E (7) Easy bushy shrub with large yellow flowers and darker

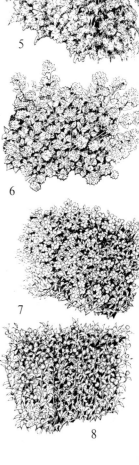

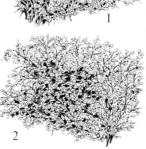

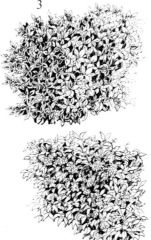

stamens from July–October. In mild winters and districts, it will also retain its leaves. Plant 45cm apart and trim in early spring. 1·8m.

Kerria japonica (8) Tough, green-stemmed, clump-forming shrub whose double egg-yolk yellow flowers open in spring. There is also a single-flowered variety and a cream and green leafed variegated form, much shorter than the type. Plant 60cm apart and trim after flowering. 1·8m. Its stems remain green throughout winter.

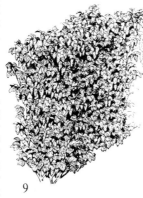
9

Ribes sanguineum (9) The hardy, tough Flowering Currant with drooping clusters of dusky red flowers in spring, seen at their richest in **'King Edward VII'** or **'Pulborough Scarlet'** forms. There is also a white-flowered form, **'Tydeman's White'**. Plant 75cm apart and trim after flowering. 2·5m.

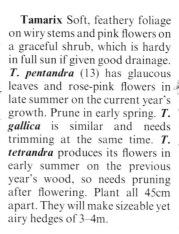
10

Rose ○ Certain groups of shrub roses make the most beautiful of all deciduous flowering hedges though they must be encouraged to become bushy at the base before developing. Cut them back hard to a few inches from the ground in the spring following planting. Thereafter prune lightly, but remove weak or dead growth. The illustration shows **'Roseraie de l'Haÿ'** (10), one of the best examples from the Rugosa rose group; it bears very fragrant, velvety, purplish-crimson large flowers with golden stamens recurrently from summer till autumn. Plant 1m apart. 2m. **'Scabrosa'** with single magenta flowers and large hips is also suitable; 1·5m. Beneath is **'Nevada'** (11) with large creamy-white semi-double flowers, massing in summer and recurrently later in the year. Plant 60cm apart. 2m. The once-flowering Alba group roses also make most

11

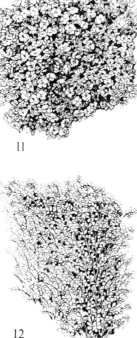
12

graceful hedges, like **'Celestial'** on p. 31. Certain hybrid musk roses are equally suitable such as **'Cornelia'** (p. 60), the flesh-pink **'Penelope'** and apricot **'Buff Beauty'**.

Symphoricarpos × doorenbosii 'Erect' (12) Clusters of showy pink-lilac berries in autumn on a compact, upright shrub which will grow in all soils. Plant 40cm apart and trim in winter. 1·8m.

Tamarix Soft, feathery foliage on wiry stems and pink flowers on a graceful shrub, which is hardy in full sun if given good drainage. **T. pentandra** (13) has glaucous leaves and rose-pink flowers in late summer on the current year's growth. Prune in early spring. **T. gallica** is similar and needs trimming at the same time. **T. tetrandra** produces its flowers in early summer on the previous year's wood, so needs pruning after flowering. Plant all 45cm apart. They will make sizeable yet airy hedges of 3–4m.

Viburnum × juddii (14) A shrub of bushy habit with fragrant pinkish-white clustered flowers in spring. Plant 40cm apart and trim after flowering. 2m. The Snowball Bush (**Viburnum opulus 'Sterile'**) (15) with its large white globes in May and autumn-colouring leaves, makes a larger, spreading hedge. Plant 75cm apart and trim after flowering. 2·5–3m. There is a golden-fruiting form of the fertile lacecap variety, **V.o. 'Xanthocarpum'** (16) which is particularly valuable in autumn.

The following are also possible for hedges: Corylus maxima 'Atropurpurea' (p. 59), Cytisus albus (p. 57), forsythia (p. 60), Hippophae rhamnoides (p. 31), philadelphus (p. 57).

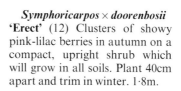

13

14

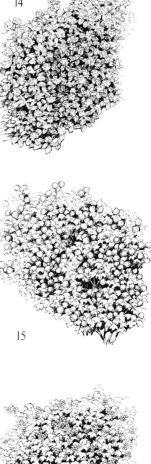
15

16

Climbers and Their Hosts

One of the most elegant ways of cultivating climbing plants is to grow them in layers. A robust, mature, stiff host plant supports a more fragile, lanky climbing plant, and in a small garden it is an ideal way of introducing diversity, for two or even three plants are grown over the same space.

Pairing the 'host' plant and its 'guest' is a matter partly of common sense, partly of knowing how each grows, and partly of aesthetic taste. Obviously both plants should enjoy the same aspect and soil. Equally obvious is the fact that the host plant should be stout and mature enough to resist being smothered by the climber enveloping it. Pair those plants which flower at different seasons and you enjoy a double display in the same area.

As for taste, some of the prettiest effects can be achieved by growing a pale and starry-flowered climber against a very dark host, such as *Solanum jasminoides* 'Album' shown garlanding a yew (*right*).

Or try rich, brilliant flowers against pale foliage (*below left*). This is *Clematis* 'Madame Grangé' supported by wires on a wall with a backcloth formed by one of the variegated ivies – *Hedera helix* 'Glacier'.

Massed berries can have an even showier effect than flowers. Here (*below right*) *Pyracantha atalantioides* 'Aurea' grows against a dark wall and the glowing gold of its fruit in autumn and winter is reinforced by trails of the yellow ivy, *Hedera helix* 'Buttercup'.

Possible host plants include cotoneaster (p. 57), berberis (p. 90), escallonia (p. 57), conifers with very small leaves like yew (p. 23), cypress (p. 91), ceanothus (p. 23), pyracantha (p. 28), *Viburnum × bodnantense* (p. 63), lilac (p. 57) and tree peony species (p. 57 and p. 60).

Climbing roses can be both hosts and guests. You might decide to grow a 'guest' climbing rose over a 'host' tree for support; here the rose 'Félicité et Perpétue' embellishes an old pear tree. Yet it will grow as well against a wall entwined by another climber. Wisteria lends itself similarly to this dual role.

Old, fruitless apple or pear trees usually make excellent hosts. So do many small trees whose outer branches dip low enough to the ground, so that the climber (planted at this outer perimeter, well out of range of the tree's greedy roots) can be trained to grow up this framework. Crab apples, laburnums and ornamental cherries are all often possible. But a truly lusty climber, like *Vitis coignetiae (below)* must be matched to an equally lofty tree, such as this larch.

Plant the climber on the sheltered side of the tree so that it is not rocked before you can train its leading shoot/s onto the tree's lower branches.

The tree doesn't even have to be alive. An old (undiseased) tree stump, or simply a pole clothed in wire netting, will provide the necessary support, rather like the individual poles of a pergola (p. 104–105). A pole can form a tall dramatic feature in a border which lacks height yet is too small for a tree. Here, *Hydrangea petiolaris* festoons the netted pole.

Screens

Screening shrubs and trees are usually planted for one of three purposes: to hide an eyesore; to act as a windbreak; or to give privacy to a garden. Plants required for the first purpose should be evergreen and ornamental – bamboos are excellent subjects, though even they tend to look tatty in a hard winter. Taller eyesores can be effectively blocked with grouped conifers, not in a line but staggered.

For use as a windbreak, trees can be evergreen or deciduous, but must be thoroughly hardy inland or, if by the sea, able to endure salt gales. Many are ultimately large and quite unsuited to the smaller garden, though the *Crataegus* species and cotoneaster listed below are useful here, as are the hollies (*Ilex*) mentioned on pages 29 and 90.

Screens planted for privacy are best selected from the evergreens listed below or under EVERGREEN HEDGES (pages 90–91). If the latter, planting distances must be increased; both Leyland cypress and *Thuja plicata*, for example, need to be planted at least 1·8m apart.

BAMBOOS AND GRASSES

Arundinaria japonica E (1) Common, very hardy bamboo tolerating windswept positions. Makes a dense screen to 4·5m. Deep green canes, leaves up to 30cm long, rich green above, part grey below. Spreads by rhizomes and sometimes invasive. Better in part-shade.

Arundinaria murieliae E (2) Most decorative clump-former with narrow green leaves on arching canes to 3m. Canes start green and yellow with age. *A. nitida* is similar, but its leaves are deeper green and canes flushed purple. Dainty appearance. Needs protection from wind. 4m.

Miscanthus saccariflorus ○ (3) Not a bamboo but a colossal, olive-green deciduous grass reaching to 2·5m when flowering in late summer to autumn. Some leaves colour well in autumn. Needs plenty of space. Useless as a winter screen – best planted where only a summer eye-catcher is required.

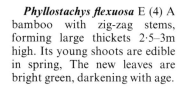

Phyllostachys flexuosa E (4) A bamboo with zig-zag stems, forming large thickets 2·5–3m high. Its young shoots are edible in spring, The new leaves are bright green, darkening with age.

SCREENING GROUPS OF TREES

Calocedrus decurrens (syn. *Libocedrus decurrens*) E (5) The Incense Cedar makes a round-topped, rich velvety-green pillar to at least 20m. Stately and impressive when grouped. Fairly rapid growth.

Chamaecyparis lawsoniana **'Pottenii'** E (6) Slim, dense columnar form of the Lawson Cypress with grey-green feathery foliage. Slow-growing to 12m.

Picea omorika E (7) Beautiful, slender, conical Serbian Spruce. Deep bluish-green leaves. Quick-growing, hardy and adapts to any soil. 20m.

Picea pungens glauca E (8) The Blue Colorado Spruce makes a slim column of stiff, blue-grey needles. Cones up to 12cm long. 20m. **'Koster'** is the most highly coloured form, but it is slow-growing to 6m.

WINDBREAK TREES: EVERGREEN AND DECIDUOUS

Acer pseudoplatanus (9) The sycamore is an outstandingly hardy tree whether inland or near the coast. Deep green leaf with pale underside. Self-sows freely. Only for very large gardens. Extremely rapid growth to 30m or more.

Alnus glutinosa (10) The common alder tolerates exposure and almost any soil (not shallow chalk), especially boggy positions. Dark green leaves and catkins in early spring. Very rapid growth to 20m. *A. incana* is also very hardy.

Cotoneaster × watereri Semi-E (11) Very hardy, semi-evergreen shrubby tree of rapid growth for smaller gardens. White flowers in spring followed by a prolific crop of red or orange-red berries. 3·5–5m.

Crataegus species. Many thorn-trees are ornamental and all are tough, bushy-headed, tolerant of any soil and situation and suitable for small gardens. *C × prunifolia* (12) has dark, glossy green leaves turning red in autumn when it also bears dark red fruit. 5m.

Cupressus macrocarpa E (13) The Monterey Cypress is a fast-growing conifer, columnar when young, spreading when mature. Best in mild or maritime areas. Grow unclipped, for it resents hard pruning. Up to 30m or more.

Pinus cembra E (14) Slow-growing, small, hardy and decorative pine. Carries deep green needles borne in fives and deep blue cones up to 8cm long. 12m.

Pinus nigra E (15) The dense, burly Austrian Pine with very dark stiff needles and cones up to 8cm long. First-class windbreak in a bleak situation whether inland or maritime. Good even in chalky soil. Only for large gardens. 30m.

Pinus ponderosa E (16) Large, very hardy, handsome pine with scaly yellow and rust-coloured bark and dark grey-green needles. Cones up to 25cm long. Only for big gardens. 30m.

Pinus radiata LH:E (17) The rapid-growing Monterey Pine with bright green needles up to 15cm long and cones up to 12cm. Picturesque but generally better suited to milder maritime exposure rather than inland. Large gardens only. 30m.

Populus alba (18) The White Poplar grows fast to around 20m. In wind, the white undersides to its glaucous leaves are conspicuous. Good in all exposed positions. An airy, dainty appearance but only for large gardens. *P. tremula* and *P. 'Robusta'* are also tough in exposed conditions. Steer clear of the Lombardy Poplar (*P. nigra 'Italica'*) which is vulnerable to wind in harsh, open situations.

Quercus cerris (19) The Turkey Oak is slender and open when young, domed when old. Dark green leaves. Good in maritime exposure rather than inland. Very rapid growth to 35m and only for large gardens.

Quercus robur (20) The English Oak, hardy to exposure whether inland or near the coast. Yellow-green leaves when new in spring (it is late to leaf), darkening to deep green. Reasonably quick growth to 35m. Only for large gardens.

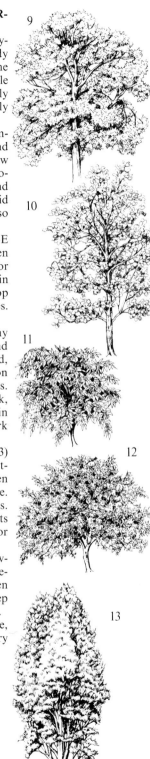

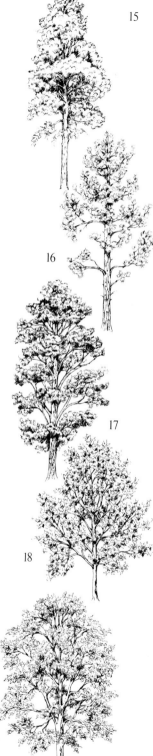

Plants for the Foot of Hedges

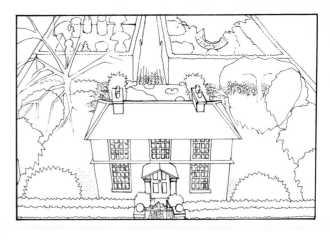

Hedges tend to be greedy-rooted creatures and the soil immediately around them is almost certain to be dry and robbed of nutrients. In a large border beside a hedge, you can leave a space between the plants and the bottom of the hedge, but where the area is only several feet, you have little option if you wish to plant it but must confine your choice to those tough, surface-rooting subjects which will tolerate poor conditions. In sun, the most suitable plants are those which enjoy a summer baking but winter shelter, and these include a number of small bulbs. In shade, only those plants which will thrive in dry shade are possibilities.

The hedge bottom must be weed-free before you establish any of the plants. Even though most are tough survivors, it is too much to expect them to cope with hedge roots *and* weeds.

BULBS

Allium moly (1) Rather invasive, small ornamental onion with glaucous leaves and golden flowers June–July. Sun or shade. 20cm. Many other small alliums are also suitable in sun, including the white or pink *A. karataviense* (2) with broad, decorative glaucous leaves and the pink, *A. ostrowskianum* (3). Both 20cm. Consider also *A. albopilosum* (syn. *A. christophii*) shown on p. 32 and *A. sphaerocephalum* (seen in Garden 1 on p. 12), though the large leaves of the former and also of *A. karataviense* are ugly when dying.

Ixia ○ (4) A South African with brilliantly coloured flowers in many shades – cream, yellow, pink, deep rose, often with a dark eye – produced in May–June–July. Full sun. In cold areas, protect in winter with ashes or bracken. 37–60cm.

Ixiolirion montanum ○ (5) Different forms bear bright blue or intense violet-blue flowers on wiry stems in early summer. Full sun. The bulbs may be offered under the names *I. ledebourii* and *I. pallasii* which are forms of the above. 30cm.

Lapeirousia cruenta (syn. *Anomatheca cruenta*) ○ (6) Flowering from summer through to late autumn, a South African bulb of fragile appearance with crimson and coral (or white) flowers among small, grassy leaves. Full sun. In cold areas, may need winter protection. 15cm.

Sternbergia lutea ○ (7) Golden flowers like a crocus in late summer–autumn and leaves which develop fully at a later stage. Full sun. 10cm. The narrow-leafed form, *S.l. angustifolia*, appears to grow and flower more freely.

Species tulips ○ Graceful bulbs most of which need a summer baking to thrive. If their position is hot and also well drained (as it should be at the foot of a hedge), they can be left to naturalise. The illustrations show *Tulipa clusiana* (8) (20cm); *T. praestans* (9) (30cm); *T. sprengeri* (11) a sound perennial and the last to flower of all tulips (rich rust-red but paler outside, 45cm) and tolerant of part shade as well as sun; *T. sylvestris* (10) (17cm); and *T. tarda* (12) a good naturaliser (10cm). See also *T. kaufmanniana* on p. 32. *T. fosteriana* (not shown) has brilliant red, huge (up to 20cm) blooms with a dark blotch at the base, but the bulbs may need lifting each year, except in hot summers.

HERBACEOUS PLANTS AND LOW SHRUBS

Anthemis cupaniana E: ○ (13) White daisy flowers most of the summer over mounds of cut silver leaves. Makes a rampant carpeter but must have full sun. 30cm × 45cm.

Asperula odorata (14) The Sweet Woodruff is also spreading but tolerant of dry shade. White starry flower heads in early summer. Scent of new-mown hay. 15cm × 30cm.

Cotoneaster dammeri E (15) Small-leaved, prostrate, evergreen shrub which will make good ground-cover. Insignificant flowers in spring and fine coral-red berries in autumn. Similar, spreading cotoneasters include **C. 'Coral Beauty'** and **C. microphylla**. 15cm × 60cm +.

Dimorphotheca barberiae (syn. *Osteospermum jucundum*) ○ (16) Dark-eyed, lilac-pink daisy flowers with grey-blue undersides produced over many months from early summer onwards. Makes spreading mats of narrow leaves. Not reliably hardy and needs full sun. Up to 30cm × 30cm.

Euphorbia robbiae E (17) Very spreading but handsome shrub with dark evergreen rosettes of leaves and, in spring to early summer, sprays of lime-green bracts rising to 60cm. Sun or shade. Plant 30cm apart.

Geranium pratense (18) Native plant with violet-blue flowers in early summer and leaves colouring well in autumn. Lusty spreader. A double form is also obtainable. 60cm × 60cm. **Geranium armenum** (syn. **G. psilostemon**) (19) is also shown with dark-eyed and very showy magenta flowers in summer. Again, leaves colour hotly in autumn. A spreader in sun. Up to 90cm × 60cm. See also the geraniums on pages 34, 64, and 70.

Hebe 'Pagei' E: ○ (20) Prostrate shrub with tiny blue-grey evergreen leaves and white flowers in early summer. Excellent ground-cover. Sun. 15cm × 40cm.

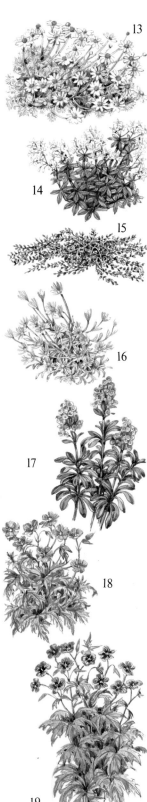

Lamium 'Beacon Silver' E: ◑ (21) Forms a spreading carpet of green-margined, metallic silver foliage with pink flowers in early to mid-summer. 10cm × 40cm. (See also *L. galeobdolon* 'Variegatum' on p. 38.)

Lunaria 'Variegata' (22) A biennial but self-sowing. The variegated form of Honesty with cream-splashed leaves and magenta flowers in early summer, followed by silvery, papery seedheads. 75cm × 30cm.

Meconopsis cambrica ○ (23) Invasively self-sowing but delicately pretty yellow or orange summer-flowering Welsh Poppy. Both single and double forms exist, though the latter can only be propagated by division. Sun. 30cm × 22cm.

Phuopsis stylosa (syn. *Crucianella stylosa*) ○ (24) Small flat heads of minute pink flowers in early summer above narrow, pointed leaves. Sun. 15cm × 30cm.

Polygonatum multiflorum (25) Graceful, arching stems bearing fresh green, ribbed leaves and small white pendulous flowers in late spring to early summer. Spreading rootstock, even in dry shade. Its popular name is the Solomon's Seal. 75cm × 30cm.

Polygonum campanulatum (26) Spreading, shallow-rooting plant with pale pink, sweet-scented flower heads produced over a long season from summer to autumn. Sun or shade. 75cm × 60cm.

Consider also: Anemones (p. 32), *Alchemilla mollis* (p. 26), *Artemisia stelleriana* (p. 30), astrantias (p. 64), *Bergenia cordifolia* (p. 26), the plain *Brunnera macrophylla* (the variegated form is shown on p. 59), *Campanula poscharskyana* (p. 25), chionodoxas (p. 32), *Chrysanthemum parthenium* 'Aureum' (p. 28), crocus (p. 33), epimediums (p. 34), *Euphorbia cyparissias* (p. 38), foxgloves (p. 38), hellebores (p. 26 and p. 62), *Iberis sempervirens* (p. 71), *Iris foetidissima* (p. 22 and p. 38), *Nerine bowdenii* (p. 33), primroses (p. 38), pulmonarias (p. 62), mossy saxifrages (p. 22), *Saxifraga fortunei* (p. 70) and *S. umbrosa* (p. 70), valerian (p. 39), *Veronica prostrata* (p. 25), vincas (p. 38), violas (p. 37), *Waldsteinia ternata* (p. 34).

Special Effects with Topiary

Nothing can equal topiary in making a garden memorable and individual, yet this living sculpture can be designed and executed without difficulty. The choice of design however, needs thought, for it can make a garden dramatic, dignified or absurd.

Very hardy evergreens with smallish leaves and a dense habit of growth are best and will ease the gardener's lot if the plants grow slowly enough to require no more than an annual clip. The ideal shrub is yew (p. 23) which will also withstand very severe clipping. But box (p. 90) is almost as good – even for intricate shapes – so is pyracantha (p. 28). Bay (p. 67) (though only truly hardy in mild areas), holly (p. 91), holm oak (p. 91), phillyrea (p. 91), *Prunus lusitanica* (p. 91) and *Viburnum tinus* (p. 91) are all excellent for simple shapes. Beech (p. 92), hawthorn (p. 92) and hornbeam (p. 92) (all deciduous) can be trained to form useful doorways and apertures in a hedge. *Lonicera nitida* (p. 22) the Lawson cypress and the Leyland cypress (both p. 91), all popular hedging subjects, grow too quickly for topiary and would require three or four trims a year.

Training

To make a design, allow the shoots of the plant to grow on until they are long enough to train. You can tie them with tarred string to a bamboo or a wire framework which will form the design. Alternatively, you could make a light wooden frame of lattice-work and the small plant's new growth can be trimmed close to the frame. Clip the trained shrub or tree at the season suggested in the text describing the plant, or in August/September if not specified. You can use either hand or electric shears for small-leafed subjects like yew and box, but secateurs are preferable for larger-leafed plants such as holly or bay whose leaves would be spoilt without individual attention. Don't clip for at least a year after planting and never clip if the branch can be trained into the shrub. Any clipping makes demands on the plant and it will need to be fed in spring with old manure or compost, bonemeal or liquid manure to keep it in peak condition.

Doorways

Although not especially ornamental in themselves, doorways are admirable tools of design in a hedged enclosure, if one can be lined up to a second door in the opposite hedge to afford a through-view. This technique was used in Garden 8. The easiest way to make a doorway is to bend over growths from the plants either side of the aperture you have left in the planting line, until they join hands, lashing them if necessary to a horizontal bamboo.

Windows

Hedge windows are not so commonly seen, but can be a valuable frame to a fine view. They need to be trained from the beginning by pinching out new growths around the intended inner frame. Early training avoids the risks attached to cutting into the main wood which might be unavoidable if you decide to hack out a window when the hedge is mature.

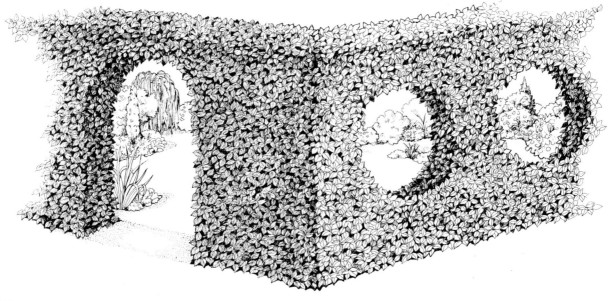

The Stilt Hedge

The simplest form of topiary is the stilt hedge. For this purpose, standard hornbeams or limes with clear stems to 1·8m are usually planted – firmly staked with a strong bamboo tied to the stake, extending the vertical line. Three or four stout horizontal bamboos are lashed to that. Distances and training of the stilt hedge are shown in the picture. The effect it makes is demonstrated in Garden 8.

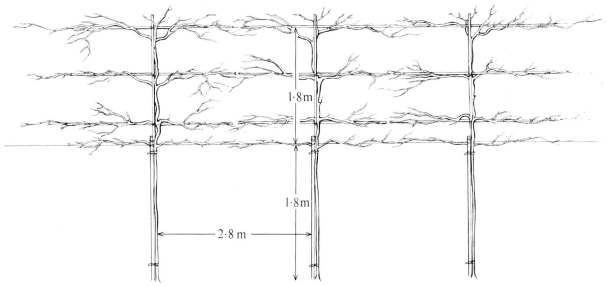

Individual Topiary Designs

Topiary forms are abundant and only a small selection of the possibilities is shown below. They range from easy geometrical forms, like a cone, to the greater complications of wedding-cakes, corkscrews and the challenging sculpture of birds, animals and even people. A simple design like the cone can be formed in three years, but even with more complex designs, good progress can be made in ten years.

Topiary Tableaux

Whole scenarios can be formed by topiary. They can be used to decorate the top of a hedge and the pictures might be figurative, symbolic or as representational as the medium will allow. Clipped shrubs are also sometimes grouped as a tableau (see Garden 8). Often impressive but nonetheless eccentric tricks played on nature, they are best displayed in a sunny, sheltered enclosure on their own.

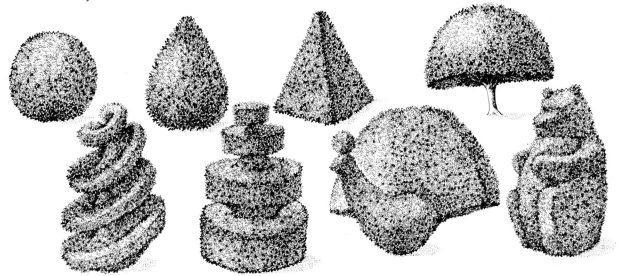

Pergolas, Pleached Alleys and Arbours

Pergolas originated in Italy where they were used as a method of growing vines until it became apparent how decoratively they could support all manner of climbing plants. Usually made from stone, brick or timber piers topped by horizontal cross-beams, they make cool, airy pathways, partly shaded in summer by their canopy of abundant foliage and flowers. At one extreme they can be installed in prosaic surroundings connecting, for example, a garage with a house door; or, shown at their most enchanting, they can form a canopy to a small bridge across water, the whole graceful structure reflected in the stream.

Suitable climbers include *Actinidia chinensis* (p. 56), in areas with warm summers *Campsis × tagliabuana* 'Madame Galen' (p. 56), clematis in variety (pp. 21, 36, 56 and 96), honeysuckles (pp. 20, 28 and 36), the golden hop (p. 28), *Jasminum officinale* (p. 36), *Solanum crispum* 'Glasnevin' (p. 21), ornamental vines (p. 21), and *Wisteria sinensis* (p. 21). Climbing roses need choosing with care since most are too tall for the verticals and will flower out of sight at the top, but 'New Dawn' and 'Schoolgirl' (p. 20) and 'Golden Showers' and 'Pink Perpétue' (p. 36) are suitable and 'Aloha' (see below) is a short pillar subject. Two other candidates make a magnificent show, one in leaf and the other in flower; *Aristolochia macrophylla* and *Wisteria floribunda* 'Macrobotrys'.

Aristolochia macrophylla Commonly called the Dutchman's Pipe on account of its 2·5–5cm bent, tubular flowers in June, it is nevertheless grown chiefly for its great, kidney-shaped leaves and tremendous vigour. Twining growth giving rapid coverage and dramatic appearance. 9m.

Climbing or shrub rose 'Aloha' ○ A short modern rose with an old-fashioned appearance due to its full pink many-petalled flowers, produced perpetually. 2m–2·5m.

***Wisteria floribunda* 'Macrobotrys'** ○ The Japanese wisteria producing stupendously long blue-purple racemes from 30cm–1m, the only reservation being that the top flowers tend to die before the bottom ones have had time to open. May–June flowering, but sometimes a few blossoms in late summer too. 4m +.

Two Examples of Pergolas

Pergola with timber verticals linked by chains (surrounded with wire), garlanded with roses.

Concrete pipes and timber concealed by *Vitis* 'Brant' and *Clematis viticella* 'Alba Luxurians'.

Pleached Alleys

Pleached alleys form a similar galleried walk to pergolas, but their actual structure differs in that it is formed from trees or large shrubs trained over strong wires, iron hoops or timber frames so that the tops of the plants interlace. Hawthorn was a favourite medieval subject; hornbeam, elm and lime attained later popularity; yew was favoured for the darkest of evergreen tunnels. In this century, laburnum has been a first choice to make this formal type of passage, its golden racemes weeping down within the framework in June. But hooped cordons of apple trees (see illustration) are almost as lovely in blossom, decorative in a second season when fruiting, of practical use, and equally effective in linking one part of the garden with another or in screening an unfortunate view.

Bowers or Arbours

Bowers or arbours are the simplest to make of these ornamental features, just summerhouses formed from climbing plants trained to cover and weep over a structure of iron or timber. The most inviting spot to build an arbour is in the sunshiny nook made between two walls, so long as it faces an engaging view.

Suitable plants are given on the previous page, but relate their habit to the size of the structure they must festoon. The wire-frame arbour shown below on the right supports *Vitis vinifera* 'Purpurea', *Clematis* 'Ville de Lyon'; pots of *Acer palmatum* 'Dissectum Atropur-pureum' and 'Pink Pearl' lilies are either side. Alternatively, an arbour can be formed from a weeping tree such as *Fraxinus excelsior* 'Pendula' (p. 89) or *Morus alba* 'Pendula', shown below on the left. This latter is the weeping form of the White Mulberry, so pendulous that the young branches must be staked up if you wish to add height to it. Its densely-packed branches, covered with large, rich green, heart-shaped leaves, will reach to the ground but can be trained over a framework. The fruits (inferior to those of the Black Mulberry) are white darkening to a pinky-red. 5m.

Planting Plan of Garden 7 (Page 84)

1. *Berberis* × *stenophylla* (p. 90)
2. *Cotoneaster* × *watereri* (p. 99)
3. *Arundinaria murieliae* (p. 98)
4. *Crataegus* × *prunifolia* (p. 99)
5. *Picea omorika* (p. 98)
6. *Populus alba* (p. 99)
7. *Rosa rugosa* 'Roseraie de l'Haÿ' (p. 95)
8. *Cotoneaster franchetii* (p. 90)
9. *Lonicera japonica* 'Halliana' (p. 20)
10. *Solanum crispum* 'Glasnevin' (p. 21)
11. Cider apple tree with *Clematis orientalis* (p. 56)
12. Cider apple tree with Rambler Rose 'Albertine' (see p. 97)
13. Cider apple tree with *Aristolochia macrophylla* (p. 104)
14. *Ceanothus* 'Delight' (p. 23)
15. Rose 'Allen Chandler' (p. 20)
16. *Pyracantha angustifolia* (p. 106)

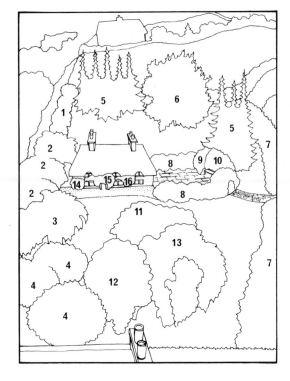

Planting Plan of Garden 8 (Page 85)

1. Hornbeam stilt hedge [Hornbeam (*Carpinus betulus*) on p. 92; stilt hedge on p. 102] underplanted with *Viola cornuta* 'Alba' and *Helleborus foetidus*, neither plant visible.
2. Dutch lavender (p. 31)
3. Laurel (*Prunus laurocerasus* 'Otto Luyken') (p. 22)
4. *Garrya elliptica* (p. 90)
5. *Azara microphylla* (p. 22)
6. *Camellia sasanqua* 'Narumi-gata' (p. 63)
7. *Prunus subhirtella* 'Pendula' (p. 19)
8. *Euphorbia robbiae* (p. 101)
9. *Cotoneaster dammeri* (p. 101)
10. *Hebe armstrongii* (p. 93)
11. *Tsuga canadensis* 'Pendula' (p. 88)
12. Helianthemum (Helianthemum in general on p. 25 and p. 39)
13. *Armeria maritima* 'Vindictive' (p. 24)
14. Yew (*Taxus baccata*) (p. 23)
15. *Cercidiphyllum japonicum* (p. 89)
16. *Bergenia cordifolia* (p. 26)
17. *Choisya ternata* (p. 22)

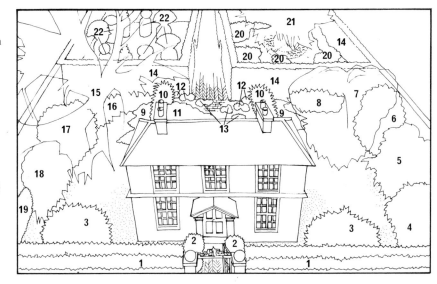

18. *Jasminum nudiflorum* (p. 63)
19. *Buxus sempervirens* 'Handsworthensis' (p. 90)
20. *Crocus tomasinianus* (p. 33)
21. *Betula jacquemontii* (p. 89)

22. Topiary yews (*Taxus baccata*) (p. 23 but see also topiary on p. 103)

Index of Plants